T0194777

An Analysis of

Max Weber's

Politics as a Vocation

William Brett with
Jason Xidias and Tom McClean

Published by Macat International Ltd
24:13 Coda Centre, 189 Munster Road, London SW6 6AW.

Distributed exclusively by Routledge
2 Park Square, Milton Park, Abingdon, Oxon OX14 4RN
711 Third Avenue, New York, NY 10017, USA

Routledge is an imprint of the Taylor & Francis Group, an informa business

www.macat.com
info@macat.com

Cataloguing in Publication Data
A catalogue record for this book is available from the British Library.
Library of Congress Cataloguing-in-Publication Data is available upon request.
Cover illustration: Etienne Gilfillan

ISBN 978-1-912303-51-9 (hardback)
ISBN 978-1-912127-67-2 (paperback)
ISBN 978-1-912282-39-5 (e-book)

Notice

The information in this book is designed to orientate readers of the work under analysis,
to elucidate and contextualise its key ideas and themes, and to aid in the development
of critical thinking skills. It is not meant to be used, nor should it be used, as a
substitute for original thinking or in place of original writing or research. References and
notes are provided for informational purposes and their presence does not constitute
endorsement of the information or opinions therein. This book is presented solely for
educational purposes. It is sold on the understanding that the publisher is not engaged
to provide any scholarly advice. The publisher has made every effort to ensure that
this book is accurate and up-to-date, but makes no warranties or representations with
regard to the completeness or reliability of the information it contains. The information
and the opinions provided herein are not guaranteed or warranted to produce particular
results and may not be suitable for students of every ability. The publisher shall not be
liable for any loss, damage or disruption arising from any errors or omissions, or from
the use of this book, including, but not limited to, special, incidental, consequential or
other damages caused, or alleged to have been caused, directly or indirectly, by the
information contained within.

CONTENTS

THE MACAT LIBRARY

The Macat Library is a series of unique academic explorations of seminal works in the humanities and social sciences – books and papers that have had a significant and widely recognised impact on their disciplines. It has been created to serve as much more than just a summary of what lies between the covers of a great book. It illuminates and explores the influences on, ideas of, and impact of that book. Our goal is to offer a learning resource that encourages critical thinking and fosters a better, deeper understanding of important ideas.

Each publication is divided into three Sections: Influences, Ideas, and Impact. Each Section has four Modules. These explore every important facet of the work, and the responses to it.

This Section-Module structure makes a Macat Library book easy to use, but it has another important feature. Because each Macat book is written to the same format, it is possible (and encouraged!) to cross-reference multiple Macat books along the same lines of inquiry or research. This allows the reader to open up interesting interdisciplinary pathways.

To further aid your reading, lists of glossary terms and people mentioned are included at the end of this book (these are indicated by an asterisk [*] throughout) – as well as a list of works cited.

Macat has worked with the University of Cambridge to identify the elements of critical thinking and understand the ways in which six different skills combine to enable effective thinking.
Three allow us to fully understand a problem; three more give us the tools to solve it. Together, these six skills make up the **PACIER** model of critical thinking. They are:

ANALYSIS – understanding how an argument is built
EVALUATION – exploring the strengths and weaknesses of an argument
INTERPRETATION – understanding issues of meaning

CREATIVE THINKING – coming up with new ideas and fresh connections
PROBLEM-SOLVING – producing strong solutions
REASONING – creating strong arguments

To find out more, visit **WWW.MACAT.COM.**

WAYS IN TO THE TEXT

KEY POINTS

- Max Weber is widely regarded as one of the founders of the field of sociology.* He also made important contributions to other fields, including political science,* history, and economics.

- The essay "Politics as a Vocation" is both a reflection on the political crisis in Germany at the time it was published in 1919, and a more general statement about the nature of modern* mass politics and the modern administrative state.

- Providing a basic understanding of politics, power, leadership, and the role of the state, the essay is one of the most groundbreaking and influential texts in the field of political science.

Who was Max Weber?

Max Weber was born in 1864 to a prominent and wealthy family in the city of Erfurt, Prussia,* a region which later became part of Germany. He was the oldest of seven children. His father was a lawyer and political figure who, soon after Max was born, moved the family to Berlin where he became a prominent National Liberal* politician.

While Weber was growing up, the German nation was under the leadership of the statesman Otto von Bismarck, and political events in

Germany influenced Weber's intellectual development throughout his life. In 1882, he went to study law at the University of Heidelberg. Two years later he left to do his military service in Strasbourg; then in 1889 he joined the University of Berlin, where he completed his studies, and also became a government consultant.

An academic and a public intellectual, Weber wanted to promote the general political education of Germans. He felt that with the end of Bismarck's rule, the country had been left with a leadership vacuum. Deep cultural and institutional change was necessary, he believed, for Germany to find the leaders it needed.

The central themes of Weber's work are: the emergence of the modern state; the links between religious doctrine* and economic models;[1] and the nature of politics and political leadership. All these themes stemmed from his involvement in German politics, and his interest in the crucial formative period of the German nation between the 1860s and 1890s.

Weber died of pneumonia in 1920 at the age of just 56, a year after the essay "Politics as a Vocation" ("*Politik als Beruf*") was published.

What Does "Politics as a Vocation" Say?

"Politics as a Vocation" developed out of a lecture Weber gave at the University of Munich in January 1919. It was published as an extended version that July, a year before his death.

As a late work, "Politics" draws on many important aspects of Weber's political and sociological thought. It is still a leading text in political science, and summarizes Weber's most important and influential thoughts on the modern political system. In it, he sets out to define politics—what it is and how it works. He also offers a good grounding in what makes good leadership, and how power functions in the modern democratic state. At the time of writing, Weber was one of Germany's most important political thinkers and commentators. Many people looked to him for advice as to how Germany should respond to the profound political crisis of the day. The country was trying to come to terms with its humbling defeat in World War I* the previous year, and many felt that revolution was a real possibility.

Weber wrote "Politics" with this situation very much in mind. The essay begins by describing how the modern bureaucratic* state started to emerge in the fourteenth and fifteenth centuries, when feudal* lords began to pay servants to carry out the work of government on their behalf. Weber then compares the democratic institutions of Germany, Great Britain and the United States as they evolved over the nineteenth century. In doing this, he draws several lessons about how modern political leaders should act. These include his argument that, from around the 1860s and 1870s onwards, Germany's bureaucracy was so large and working for it was so prestigious, that ambitious people tended to choose careers in government departments rather than in parliament. The strength of German bureaucracy, in other words, actually created a significant shortage of experienced political leaders.

Weber also outlines the qualities those leaders would need. He feels they should be visionaries who live *for* politics rather than live *from* it. He identifies three sorts of authority: the traditional authority* of the feudal lords; the authority that comes from personal charisma; and the "rational legal" kind of authority* that relies on the belief that those in power are there for good, logical reasons. For Weber, the kind of leader a modern democracy needs is someone with charismatic authority.*

Weber also outlines his views on how politicians should act in relation to the state of affairs in Germany at the time. Instead of proposing concrete solutions, he looks at the fundamental features of modern politics, arguing that the country needed to balance its strong state with mature political leadership. This maturity would call for leaders with the ability to balance strong moral convictions with a practical approach—charismatic leaders, that is, who could compromise. Any government would need to work with society as it actually was, rather than with an ideal of how it might be.

In this sense, Weber's views stood in stark contrast to those of his fellow countryman and philosopher Karl Marx.* Marxism* made a case for a utopian* (idealistic) vision in which the working class would—and should—rise up and topple the ruling class. The upheaval and destruction this would involve was seen as necessary to achieve the goal.

Why Does "Politics as a Vocation" Matter?

"Politics as a Vocation" was a pioneering text in both political science and, to a lesser extent, sociology. Weber is regarded as one of the three founders of sociology, along with Karl Marx and the French thinker Émile Durkheim.*[2] He also had an important influence on political science, history, and economics, and on sub-fields such as religious studies. Even in his day, he was an extremely influential scholar, and "Politics" contains a summary of his life's work. Although his views were not debated much in the period after his death in 1920, social scientists rekindled interest in them in the 1960s, and Weber's theories have since gone on to have enormous impact. His ideas on the nature of politics, power, the state, political rule, and political leadership are now so central to the academic disciplines of political science and political sociology that people sometimes forget that they originally came from him.

Weber's historical analysis of how the modern state developed has inspired many important thinkers, and many of his concepts are still relevant today. His theories on what makes for effective politics are often viewed as essential learning for undergraduates. Scholars, meanwhile, focus on key ideas such as:

- the definition of the modern state as an organization that enjoys a monopoly on legitimate force in a given territory.

- the different types of legitimate authority: traditional, charismatic, and rational/legal.

- rationalization*—the decline of rule by traditional authority figures like lords, and the rise of societies organized around bureaucratic states and rational efficiency—as a fundamental feature of modernity.

"Politics as a Vocation" also introduces Weber's definition of the state as a body that successfully claims that it, alone, can legitimately use force in a particular territory. This idea has become central to contemporary political thinking.

However, Weber's greatest influence on contemporary scholarship does not stem from the concepts he describes in "Politics," or his interests, but from the method he uses to make his argument. This is the comparative historical method* in which he compares the development of particular policies in different societies.

We now live in an age of great disengagement from and disillusionment with politics. People around the world are disappointed in political leadership, and angry about failed public policies and corruption. This contemporary context has helped Weber's ideas remain relevant far beyond the particular political landscape of Germany in 1919, in which he first published his thoughts.

NOTES

1 Max Weber, *The Protestant Ethic and the Spirit of Capitalism* (New York: Routledge, 2001).

2 David Owen and Tracy B. Strong, eds., introduction to *The Vocation Lectures* by Max Weber (Indianapolis, IN: Hackett, 2004) x.

SECTION 1
INFLUENCES

MODULE 1
THE AUTHOR AND THE HISTORICAL CONTEXT

KEY POINTS

- Providing an influential account of modern* politics, power, leadership, and the role of the state, the essay "Politics as a Vocation" is a defining text in the field of political science.*

- Weber's upbringing in a business-oriented family with an interest in politics shaped his vision of how Germany should be governed.

- The essay was written in 1919 against the backdrop of Germany's defeat in World War I* and the founding of the Weimar Republic.*

Why Read this Text?

Max Weber first delivered "Politics as a Vocation" ("*Politik als Beruf*") in the original German, as a lecture to the student union of the University of Munich on January 28, 1919. Although he was already a renowned public intellectual, the lecture was a prominent event that helped to cement his reputation further.[1]

The essay is often paired with another lecture that Weber gave the year before, entitled "Science as a Vocation." These texts, collectively called "The Vocation Lectures," were written for an educated public audience and contain summaries of some of the most important aspects of Weber's overall thought. They also demonstrate how serious scholarly understanding might be applied to practical problems. In the case of "Politics," the pressing practical problem was: how can a fully modern society emerge at a time of great turbulence? Germany had

> 66 Max Weber has claim not only to be one of the
> founding fathers of modern social science but also
> to being one of the most acute diagnosticians of the
> conditions of modernity in the West. 99
>
> Machiavelli, *The Prince* David Owen* and Tracy B. Strong,* introduction to
> *The Vocation Lectures*

just lost World War I and was in the middle of serious social upheaval.

Today, "Politics as a Vocation" is widely regarded as a groundbreaking and influential text in the field of political science. It serves as a foundation for understanding what politics is—that is, what constitutes good political leadership, how politics relates to power, how power is concentrated in the modern democratic state, and the importance of the art of compromise in political decision-making.

Author's Life

Weber was born in 1864 in the Prussian* city of Erfurt (now part of Germany). His father was a prominent businessman who moved the family to Berlin soon after Max was born and entered politics as a member of the National* Liberal* Party. This provided the young Max with status and the chance to engage politically from an early age. But he wasn't the only one in the family to do so. His brother Alfred also became an influential sociologist* and political scientist.

Weber trained in the social sciences, specializing in law, at the University of Heidelberg and the University of Berlin. He took up his first academic appointment at the University of Freiberg in 1894. Just two years later, he moved on to the University of Heidelberg, where he was appointed Professor of Political Economy. It was there that he established his reputation as a brilliant intellectual. However, Weber did not engage with the important questions of his day solely as an academic. He was also a consultant to the government, and a co-founder of the liberal German Democratic Party.* He participated in negotiations over the 1919 Treaty of Versailles,* the peace treaty that officially ended the war between Germany and the Allied Powers, although he was actually opposed to Germany signing it. He also contributed to the drafting of the constitution of the Weimar Republic,* the democratic system that Germany opted for in 1919.

Author's Background

When Weber delivered the lecture version of "Politics as a Vocation" on January 28, 1919, Germany was in serious turmoil as a result of the country's defeat in World War I and the collapse of the German Empire.* The situation was highly unstable. The newly formed national assembly,* led by the Social Democratic Party,* was threatened by both right-wing nationalists* and left-wing communists.* Rosa Luxemburg* and Karl Liebknecht*—key figures in the more radical section of the German socialist* movement—had been assassinated 13 days before, and the political atmosphere was extremely heated.

In this turbulent setting Weber employed all his knowledge of sociology, economics, and history to make a strong statement about the nature and potential of political power in modern societies. In "Politics" he describes the importance of having a strong, charismatic political leader who is willing to use a combination of personal conviction and authority to construct a stable and mature regime. The lecture can be seen as an indirect reflection on some core institutional and cultural features of German politics that Weber thought had contributed to the political crisis. These included the dominance of the bureaucracy* of government over party politics, and a tendency to pursue certain goals whatever the cost, on the assumption that the end always justifies the means.

Weber was a member of the German business-owning bourgeoisie,* and is often portrayed as both the representative and advocate[2] of the middle classes. He believed that German industrialization*—the process of moving from an agricultural to an industrial society—had not helped establish a politically competent middle class, as it had in Great Britain. This process had been quicker and had come later in Germany than it had in Britain, and had also differed in its social foundations. In Britain, industrialization happened with little involvement of the monarchy* (the king or queen) or the aristocracy* (men and women who enjoy high status in a society thanks to their "noble" birth.) This weakened their power, because it gave birth to a new class of rich capitalists. In Germany, however, industrialization was overseen by a powerful central figure, the statesman Otto von Bismarck,* and occurred in cooperation with the aristocratic ruling class rather than independently from it. As a result, industrialization in Germany reinforced the power of the authoritarian political system and the administrative state.

Weber argues that the bureaucratic system of government provided an appealing, prestigious career for ambitious young members of the bourgeoisie. Perhaps this reflected his background. In contrast, a career in parliament did not offer good opportunities and could lead to conflict with the Kaiser* and his ministers—the aristocrats who held the *real* power. As a result, unlike other European countries—especially Great Britain—Germany did not have institutions that encouraged competent leaders to emerge. Weber's main aim in "Politics as a Vocation" was to highlight this problem. He wanted to foster the formation of political institutions that would help to develop the sort of leadership he believed was essential for a modern nation state.

NOTES

1   David Owen and Tracy B. Strong, introduction to *The Vocation Lectures* by Max Weber (Indianapolis, IN: Hackett, 2004) ix.

2   In 1926, he was described somewhat dismissively as the "bourgeois Marx" by a fellow German sociologist, Albert Salomon.

MODULE 2
ACADEMIC CONTEXT

KEY POINTS

- Max Weber's essay "Politics as a Vocation" contributed to our understanding of the nature of politics and political rule in relation to the modern* state.

- Although Weber was influenced by the philosophy of Karl Marx* and Friedrich Nietzsche,* he did not share their vision of politics and society.

- Weber's arguments fit into the broad intellectual tradition known as "liberalism."*

The Work In Its Context

Weber wrote the essay "Politics as a Vocation" for a popular, rather than an academic, audience. An important and influential text nonetheless, it condenses Weber's own scholarly work and applies it to a problem that he believed was relevant to his immediate audience. The essay should be considered in the context of his own earlier work on politics, rather than the work of other scholars.

"Politics" was written at a time when the disciplines of sociology* (the study of the forces and structures that form and shape human societies) and political science* (the study of politics and the workings of governments) were in their infancy.

Until the publication of "Politics," the study of what we now call political science was almost entirely concerned with formal institutions. First, scholars would describe the features of a political institution—a constitution, or a parliament, for example. Or they would describe the features of an established practice, like traditional privilege. They would then examine all these things from a theoretical

> **❝ It might be a basic characteristic of existence that those who would know it completely would perish, in which case the strength of a spirit should be measured according to how much of the 'truth' one could still barely endure. ❞**
> Friedrich Nietzsche, "Beyond Good and Evil"

perspective. Little attention was paid to how these institutions actually worked in practice, or whether they were effective in meeting their intended purpose.

Weber's insistence that scholars should try to understand how people actually behaved in relation to these institutions and practices, and why they acted the way they did, was a novel way of applying sociological techniques to the subject of politics.

Overview of the Field

People tend to see Weber's political scholarship as being grounded primarily in liberalism—a political philosophy that emphasizes the importance of individual freedom of belief, speech, and association. Liberalism was an intellectual movement that emerged after the establishment of a constitutional monarchy* in Great Britain in the second half of the seventeenth century, and after the French and American Revolutions* of the late eighteenth century.

Beyond liberalism, Weber's work was also shaped and influenced by Marxism* and the philosophy of Friedrich Nietzsche. Because he accepted some of their proposals and rejected others, he should not be thought of as a strict disciple of any of these grand intellectual currents. It was his critical approach and originality that cemented his reputation as a foundational thinker in the field of modern social science. Indeed, Weber's entire body of work can be seen as a critical response to Marxism.

Both Weber and Marx were concerned with modernity, capitalism,* and social order. For Marx, historical change could be explained via a critical examination of the structure and operation of the economy and, to a lesser extent, the relationship between the economy and legal institutions. Marx emphasized the way in which processes of economic production were organized, and identified the difference between those who *owned* things like factories, tools, and machinery, and those who were paid to *work* them as particularly important. This is what he termed the "means of production."

Weber drew on the work of Friedrich Nietzsche too, particularly on his idea of the importance of heroic individuals—the "superman" (übermensch). These supermen are people of such extraordinary moral worth that they are able to transcend slavish obedience to established patterns of behavior. In this way their actions serve as an example to the masses.

Academic Influences

Weber's nuanced relationship with these three influences (liberalism, Marxism and Nietzsche) produced what has been described by the British sociologist Anthony Giddens as a "massive, but brittle, intellectual synthesis of Marx and Nietzsche."[1]

Although we can tell from his political writing that Weber was personally committed to liberalism, as an academic he insisted on examining the way in which politics and power actually worked in practice, regardless of how "good" or "bad" any political institution might be. For example, he freely admitted that the institutions of the modern bureaucratic* state have an unprecedented ability to regulate society and achieve political goals. It is easy to assume from these statements that he took a positive, rather than a neutral, view of this—which put him at odds with certain liberal thinkers. Indeed, Weber did not believe that bureaucratization could be reversed; he foresaw a future in which its spread would slowly extinguish practical opportunities for people to exercise their freedom. It was analysis like this that prompted the German historian Theodor Mommsen* to describe Weber as a "liberal in despair."[2]

Weber's response to Marx, meanwhile, was also complex. Where Marx believed that there were laws that applied to all societies and communities alike, Weber noted that different societies took different routes depending on the events and local processes that affected them. And although he acknowledged that economic factors were important, Weber thought that the social relations within an economy were at least as important as things such as who got paid to do the labor and how the profits were shared.

He also claimed that Marx's focus on the ownership of the means of production was a mistake. He pointed out that capitalists' ownership of the means of production was only one instance of a broader trend: the increasingly widespread reliance on bureaucracy.

Weber believed that power came from control over bureaucratic organizations, whether they be large firms, political parties or government departments, rather than the ownership of economically productive resources. Reading "Politics as a Vocation," this emphasis on bureaucratization is central to Weber's "dispute" with Marx.

Max Weber's debt to Nietzsche, meanwhile, is most clearly seen in the emphasis he places on the importance of charismatic authority* as a counterbalance to bureaucratic authority.

NOTES

1   Anthony Giddens, *Politics and Sociology in the Thought of Max Weber* (London: Macmillan, 1972), 58.

2   W. J. Mommsen and M. Steinberg, *Max Weber and German Politics, 1890–1920* (Chicago: University of Chicago Press, 1990).

THE PROBLEM

KEY POINTS

- In "Politics as a Vocation," Weber asks the questions, "What is politics?" and "How should politicians act, given the way things are in Germany?"
- Weber's work draws on diverse scholarly literature and intellectual movements, including classical and modern* political philosophy and sociology.*
- In contrast to Karl Marx,* Weber argues for a strong ruling class.

Core Question

In his essay "Politics as a Vocation," Max Weber was not trying to start a new academic debate. Instead, he wanted to make an informed contribution to the contemporary political debate by answering the question, "How should political leaders act, given the fundamental nature and constraints of modern politics?"

In asking this question, Weber was attempting to go beyond a superficial examination of what the "best" political policies were in relation to Germany's problems at the time. He was not, in other words, arguing on behalf of socialist,* liberal,* or conservative policies—even if that was probably what his audience most wanted from him.

Instead, he was interested in understanding how somebody of any political persuasion should go about the business of politics in general. This was important, he believed, because many German politicians seemed to assume that "doing politics well" involved pursuing their chosen political ends, regardless of what it might cost the nation.

> ❝ Returning to Munich in late 1918, Weber observed the Revolution in Germany with dismay. The 'bloody carnival', as he called it, simply weakened Germany in its moment of defeat. ❞
>
> Peter Lassman* and Ronald Speirs,* introduction to *Weber: Political Writings*

The importance of "Politics as a Vocation" to public discussion lay in the way it combined two separate questions—indeed, two separate *kinds* of question. The first was a *normative** question (how should things be?). This was perhaps of greatest interest to his immediate audience. The second was an *empirical** question (why are things the way they are?).

His answer to this second question has proven to be of enduring relevance to the scholars who followed him.

The Participants

Wanting to redefine the terms of the debate, Weber rarely names other participants. Nor does he lay out their positions. It is clear, though, that he is arguing against three main sets of opponents: conservatives who sought a return to the authoritarian status quo of the pre-war years; Marxist* revolutionaries who thought their utopian* ideals should be achieved at any cost; and liberals who refused to acknowledge that Germany did not have political leaders capable of overcoming the challenges the country faced.

These nameless people only appear in the essay indirectly. And the only reason they are present is because they believed that "doing politics well" was a matter of having firm convictions and sticking to them, regardless of the cost to themselves or others, or because they failed to appreciate the ethical dilemmas that are a fundamental and inescapable part of modern politics. Their anonymity is all the more stark given that, in the final part of the essay, Weber seeks to show their political naivety by citing ethical thinkers as notable as Aristotle,* Jesus Christ, and Machiavelli.*

The Contemporary Debate

The arguments that Weber lays out in the essay were eclipsed both by the author's death soon after it was published, and by the political turmoil that Germany experienced over the following two decades. As a result, the text did not immediately form part of any academic debate on the specific subjects it raised. It did, however, contribute to scholarly discussion and inquiry more broadly: first, in relation to the political philosophy of Karl Marx, and second, in relation to the nature of modern democracy.

Weber responds to Marx's assertion that class conflict is at the root of the historical development of society. He argues that the modern state has developed according to the fluctuating resources and power of aristocrats* and the bourgeoisie* (for Marx, those men and women of the middle class who own and manage capitalist* production).

It has been argued that Weber differs from Marx in the philosophical purpose of his work.[1] Marx sought to encourage class consciousness* among the working class; he wanted to make working people understand that they, themselves, play a role in the continuation of a system that robs them of their power. As a member of the bourgeoisie himself, Weber wanted to help his class to a mature understanding of what political action and leadership might entail. Marx tended to downplay the role of political leadership in shaping the future of society. However, "Politics" concludes with a call for political maturity in order to foster strong national leadership.

The essay has also contributed to discussion related to the role and potential of modern democracy. At the time of its publication, the most influential tradition in this field was that of liberal democratic theory,* which advocated widespread public participation in government and politics.[2] This remains a very important tradition today.

Weber, however, viewed the idea that the masses can actually play a direct role in politics or government as deeply unrealistic, regardless of whether it was desirable in principle. Arguments over the purpose and ideal shape of political institutions, and how the public is involved in them, continue to run along similar lines; "Politics as a Vocation" has come to be seen as a foundational text in the "elitist" school* of thought, which argues that social affairs are controlled by small groups of elites.

NOTES

1   See David Beetham, *Max Weber and the Theory of Modern Politics* (London: George Allen & Unwin, 1974), 241.

2   Robert Dahl, *Democracy and its Critics* (Yale: Yale University Press, 1989).

MODULE 4
THE AUTHOR'S CONTRIBUTION

KEY POINTS

- "Politics as a Vocation" sets out to explore the features of modern* politics, and then to draw lessons about how those who aspire to be leaders should act.

- Max Weber contributed to our understanding of what politics is, how it relates to power and the state, and what constitutes political leadership.

- While Weber drew from classical and modern political philosophy and empirical sociology* (that is, the study of social science based on the interpretation of measurable evidence), the arguments he made were largely original.

Author's Aims

In his essay "Politics as a Vocation," Max Weber's stated aim was to explain "what politics is as a vocation and what it can mean."[2] This statement sets out two related aims—one practical and material; the other ethical.

Weber claimed he would explain the fundamental features of modern politics. From this he would draw ethical lessons for people who saw political leadership as their calling in life. He wanted to outline enduring lessons for all leaders, regardless of their politics; whether conservative, liberal,* socialist* or of some other political persuasion, how should they act? His aim was to avoid topics of contemporary political interest, despite the fact that his immediate audience was caught up in political turmoil of revolutionary proportions.

> ❝ Only he has the calling for politics who is sure that he
> will not crumble when the world from his point of view
> is too stupid or base for what he wants to offer. Only he
> who in the face of all this can say 'In spite of all!' has the
> calling for politics. ❞
>
> Max Weber, "Politics as a Vocation"[1]

The text of "Politics as a Vocation" was first offered as a lecture at the University of Munich in 1919 to an audience of radical students and bourgeois* figures such as the poet Rainer Maria Rilke* and the psychiatrist and philosopher Karl Jaspers.* Weber was perhaps the best-known and most respected public intellectual in Germany, and the lecture was regarded as a major event. Many Germans looked to Weber for answers to their nation's problems.[3]

Approach

Weber's approach to the essay's major question—"What is politics as a vocation and what can it mean?"—was unusual. He based an ethical argument on observable evidence. His insistence on examining fundamental issues of political leadership in general, rather than being drawn into a one-sided argument, was equally unusual.

The text begins by defining a few key terms. The first is "politics," which is described as collective action oriented towards the state—a matter of winning control over the state and using its power to achieve a goal.

Next, it defines the "state" as an organization that "successfully claims a monopoly over the legitimate use of physical force in a given territory." Weber highlights the essentially violent nature of the state early in the lecture, because it has significant consequences for the ethical argument he makes at the end.

He then discusses the term "vocation" at some length, noting both its almost religious sense of "one's calling in life" and its more practical sense of "the way one earns a living." This dual meaning also proves significant to his final argument.

The task that Weber sets himself, therefore, is to understand how politicians—those who want to win and use the power of the state—should act. He does this in the context of the state, and of modern politics more generally.

First, he engages in an extended historical analysis of how modern political institutions emerged from the societies of the fourteenth and fifteenth centuries. He argues that this was, in essence, a process by which the institutions of government administration became bureaucratized. He then examines how politics was "done" in the late nineteenth century in a few modern Western states—Great Britain, the United States, France and Germany. He pays particular attention to the historical development of modern mass democracy, the most important aspect being the gradual extension of the right to vote to all adult males. But Weber also discusses parliaments and their committees, the office of president, and political parties. Doing this, he sets out what a more recent commentator has called the "external realities of the political realm."[4]

In the final part of the lecture, Weber explores the ethical implications of these empirical* facts. He reiterates the claim he made at the start—that the bureaucratic* state is essentially an institutionalized form of violence—and emphasizes the impact of differing institutional forms of modern mass democracy. He identifies the ethical attitudes and personal characteristics that aspiring leaders need in order to deal with these facts and to "do" politics well: charisma balanced with authority over the bureaucratic machine; and an ability to balance personal commitment with an awareness of the impact of the violence that might be required for progress to be achieved.

Contribution In Context

The breadth and originality of Weber's political thought—a consequence of his lifetime's work as a historian, economist, political scientist,* and sociologist—can be seen in the sections he writes on bureaucracy, on the emergence of the modern world and society's turn towards rational thought, institutions and social habits.

It can also be seen in the pages he writes on the three forms of "legitimate authority:" traditional (authority rising from customary obedience); charisma (authority arising from a politician's personal charm) and "rational legal"* (the authority invested in any leader to lead in accordance with the law).

Weber's ideas, however, were also influenced by the work of one of his former students, Robert Michels,* especially the book *Political Parties: A Sociological Study of the Oligarchical Tendencies of Modern Democracy*.[5] Michels published this seminal study of how political parties function and evolve in 1911.

Weber adopted many of the arguments put forward by Michels—in particular, the idea that, since modern political parties are bureaucratic organizations, they usually fall under the control of a small number of highly involved party officials. Once this happens, the party becomes less responsive to the wishes of its members. Weber did not, however, agree with Michels's conclusion that they are therefore incompatible with democracy.* While he did not deny that parties tend to become "oligarchical" (run by and for the benefit of a small number of people), he nevertheless believed them to be necessary in political systems where everyone is able to vote, because there is no other effective way to mobilize large numbers of citizen-voters. Whatever their faults, Weber reasoned, bureaucratically organized parties did allow people to engage with politics in large numbers.

NOTES

1   Max Weber, "Politics as a Vocation," in *The Vocation Lectures*, eds. David Owen and Tracy B. Strong (Indianapolis, IN: Hackett, 2004), 93–4.

2   Max Weber, "Politics as a Vocation," 32.

3   Tracy B. Strong, *Politics Without Vision* (Chicago: University of Chicago Press, 2012), 133–6.

4   Owen and Strong, introduction to *The Vocation Lectures* by Max Weber (Indianapolis, IN: Hackett, 2004.

5   Robert Michels, *Political Parties: A Sociological Study of the Oligarchical Tendencies of Modern Democracy* (New Brunswick, NJ: Transaction Publishers, 1999).

SECTION 2
IDEAS

MODULE 5
MAIN IDEAS

KEY POINTS

- The modern state requires rational, bureaucratic*
  organization and a charismatic, bourgeois* leader who can
  mobilize the masses.

- Weber looks at how the bureaucratic state has developed
  in different countries and how leaders should learn how to
  lead.

- Weber expects his readers to have some knowledge of
  political terms, while also introducing new concepts of his
  own, such as "rationalization."*

Key Themes

Max Weber's essay "Politics as a Vocation" is essentially about political power in modern societies. The text's key concepts all relate to aspects of this power.

To Weber, social power lies in physical violence. That is to say, he believes that social power in its most basic form consists of physically compelling others to do what you want. He defines the state as the institution that successfully "claims the monopoly of legitimate physical violence within a particular territory."[1]

In most societies, however, those in power rarely need to resort to physical violence to make the people do what they want. They rule, rather, by means of "domination" or "authority." Weber points to three different kinds of authority: "traditional authority,"* "charismatic authority,"* and "rational-legal authority."*

"Traditional authority" is based on "unimaginably ancient and habitual" obedience; "charisma" is the capacity to inspire personal

> ❝ Politics means a slow, powerful drilling through hard boards with a mixture of passion and a sense of proportion. ❞
>
> Max Weber, "Politics as a Vocation"

devotion or confidence in the unique qualities of the leader;"'"rational legal" authority lies in the people's belief that those in power have been elevated according to rational and legal procedures, and that they use their authority using rules that have been established in similar ways.

Exploring The Ideas

Weber's essay puts these concepts to use in a three-part argument. First, he explains the origins of institutions that allow people to earn a living from being involved in politics. The first institution to emerge was the modern bureaucratic state in the fourteenth and fifteenth centuries. Before that, feudal* lords governed using their own money and resources, which allowed them to act somewhat independently of the "prince" above them. Eventually, however, the ruling princes used their own resources to take power from the aristocratic* classes by employing servants to carry out the business of government on their behalf. Over time, this stimulated the growth of ministries, or state departments, which employed experts to collect taxes and to wage war for the princes. Bureaucracy proved so effective that all princes who wanted to remain in power had to adopt it.

In the second part of Weber's argument, he conducts a comparative historical analysis* of democratic institutions in Great Britain, the United States and Germany. His aim is to show how different historical circumstances affect opportunities for aspiring leaders to develop skills and gain the experience they need.

In Britain there was a long-standing tradition of effective government by parliament.* Most local administration was already carried out by men of high social status (the "gentry") and that encouraged those with real political ambition to focus on parliament, where power and the opportunities for advancement lay. So parliamentary government discouraged the development of a large independent bureaucracy. This explains why, even before the advent of mass democracy in the mid-nineteenth century, Britain had already had great leaders such as William Gladstone,* a politician elected to the position of prime minister four times.

In the United States, however, mass democracy was established *before* the development of strong parties. This, combined with the presidency, led to the "spoils" system in the US, where candidates promised to give jobs to supporters as a reward for electoral support. Weber argues that this slowed the development of a professional civil service and weakened the political value of leadership.

In Germany, politically ambitious people tended to choose careers in prestigious government ministries rather than in parliament—that is, in administration rather than in crafting laws and policy. Bureaucrats do not make good politicians, and Germany in the early twentieth century lacked mature, experienced political leaders.

In the third part of his argument, Weber identifies several ethical conflicts that mature leaders must overcome. First, leaders must live "for" politics, in the sense of being personally committed to a particular vision; they must exercise a fundamentally charismatic kind of authority. Though to win office at all, they must command obedience from bureaucratic organizations, such as their own party.

Second, leaders must make compromises with regard to the vision that brought them to office. This is the ethical thing to do. To show why, Weber distinguishes between two approaches to politics: the "ethic of ultimate ends" (which judges the merits of a political program on the basis of the goals it seeks to achieve), and the "ethic of responsibility" (which recognizes that the world is imperfect and anticipates that even good policies can have unintended or harmful consequences). For Weber, the only acceptable course is an ethics of responsibility. The principal tool for achieving political goals—the state—is inherently violent. However, it is morally unacceptable and self-defeating to assume that good policies should be pursued even if they have bad effects.

Language And Expression

"Politics as a Vocation" is a dense text that contains some political jargon. Weber assumed that his target audience was familiar with political and sociological concepts.

He also assumed that his readers were aware of current events in Germany, like the revolutionary feeling that followed its defeat in World War I.* He also expected them to be familiar with German institutions such as the *Reichsbank**—the central bank—and with figures such as the British Prime Minister Benjamin Disraeli.* He refers to these things freely, without giving his audience background. Presumably most educated Germans of the time would have been informed enough to follow easily.

Weber also coined some jargon of his own. Perhaps the most important for "Politics" is "rationalization," which refers to the process by which traditional forms of authority—feudal lordship, clan rule, village elders, and so on—were gradually replaced by rational-legal forms of authority, including departments of state, political parties, and corporations. For Weber, rationalization is a fundamental part of development in the modern world. It is the reason why political power today rests on a combination of legality (the enforcement of rules by a senior official in a large bureaucratic organization), and charisma (a leader's personal prestige, which encourages supporters to follow his or her rules).

These ideas, like Weber's definition of the state as holding "the monopoly of legitimate physical violence within a particular territory,"[2] are considered to be extremely influential concepts.

NOTES

1   Max Weber, "Politics as a Vocation," in *The Vocation Lectures*, ed. David Owen and Tracy B. Strong (Indianapolis, IN: Hackett, 2004), 33.

2   Weber, "Politics as a Vocation," 33.

MODULE 6
SECONDARY IDEAS

KEY POINTS

- "Politics as a Vocation" is notable for the "comparative historical method" that Weber used; his distinction between traditional,* charismatic,* and legal authority* remains an influential concept in political science to the present day.

- Weber distinguishes between "those who live from politics" and "those who live for politics."

- Weber offers a discussion of the pros and cons of presidential* and parliamentary* systems of government—as well as comments on the inherent difficulties of being in politics—that may be considered a precursor to modern debates on the subject.

Other Ideas

In addition to the essay's discussion of the nature of political power, Max Weber's "Politics as a Vocation" is notable for two secondary elements: its methodological approach (which we can call comparative sociology*), and the way it defines different types of legitimate authority.

"Politics as a Vocation" gives examples of three aspects of Weber's social-scientific approach. First, he discusses legitimacy, outlining three "ideal types"* of legitimate authority: traditional, charismatic, and rational-legal. These "ideal types" are conceptual notions, or constructs. They correspond to aspects of the social world, but exaggerate key characteristics. They do not conform exactly to things that can be seen in the real world, but are used as tools for ordering and understanding them.

Second, the essay's historical reading of political institutions clearly

> ** ❝ Either one lives 'for' politics or one lives 'off' politics. ❞ **
> Max Weber, "Politics as a Vocation"

demonstrates Weber's distinctive method of comparative sociology. He seeks explanations for social realities and how they emerged, and compares the emergence of similar phenomena in different places. He examines the development of modern political institutions in Britain, the United States, and Germany to explain how each institution produced a different kind of political leadership.

There is also a third aspect to Weber's method. Although not quite as obvious in "Politics" as in some of his other works, it deserves a mention because it has been the subject of considerable debate among social scientists. Weber believed that scientific knowledge of society was possible, but that social action can only be understood with reference to the meaning that people give it. Social science, therefore, has to be based on a very significant degree of what Weber terms *verstehen*: interpretation or understanding. This contrasts with some of the ideas of positivism* and neoclassical economics.*

According to the positivist position, knowledge of society may only be gleaned from analysis of observable phenomena (that is, from *behavior* rather than *beliefs*, which cannot be directly observed), and society, much like the natural world, is subject to certain impersonal laws. It is the job of social scientists to discover what these laws are.

Neoclassical economics, which is based on the explicit assumption that individuals always seek to act rationally in pursuit of their own self-interest, is one of the most prominent examples of this positivist approach in contemporary politics and scholarly work.

Exploring The Ideas
Weber tries to explain why people might voluntarily submit to authority (by, for example, obeying commands to do things they

might not otherwise do). He argues that obedience is a result of "legitimacy"—the belief that the person giving orders has the right to do so. He then identifies the three "ideal types" of legitimate authority: traditional, charismatic, and rational-legal.

Traditional authority rests on a belief in long-established practices, habits and other traditions. A good example occurs in an absolute monarchy,* under which authority is passed on from one generation to another through hereditary succession.* For Weber, the emergence of the modern* world was largely a process of replacing traditional authority with other forms, especially legal authority.

Charismatic authority rests on a belief in the special characteristics of the person in authority. Although Weber appears to have had prophets and the founders of religions in mind in developing this ideal type, he was also referring to modern politicians who inspire personal devotion among their followers and the electorate at large.

"Legal authority" is respected when people obey because they believe the person in authority to have been granted the power to give orders as a result of a formal, orderly process consistent with abstract principles. The archetypal example of this kind of authority figure is the bureaucrat.*

Weber believes that these ideal types can and do overlap considerably, in practice. Indeed, his argument about the ethical challenges of modern leadership is based, in part, on the claim that great leaders must simultaneously exercise two different, and often contradictory, types of power: charismatic and rational-legal.

Overlooked

Later scholarship paid little attention to the part of the text that may have been most important to Weber himself: his account of the conditions that must be met by political figures if they are to act well, and his insight into the ethical challenges of politics in the modern world. There is an exception to this, however: some critics claimed that

Weber's analysis contributed to the development of fascism* in Germany. His focus on the need for an almost heroically charismatic political leader is sometimes seen as an intellectual precursor to the rise of Nazism.*[1]

Yet if Weber's views on leadership and political action are taken out of their historical context and applied to current political problems, they have a more optimistic application.

There is a widespread and growing mistrust of politicians and politics in developed democracies.[2] Some believe this is a serious threat to the very legitimacy and sustainability of democratic societies. This mistrust has been at least partly put down to a misunderstanding by many people of the nature of political rule, and the degree to which politics is by nature a difficult and complicated occupation. Theorists such as the British political scientist David Runciman* have suggested that a better recognition of these difficulties could help people to come to terms with the problems of democratic politics.[3] This, they argue, would make an important contribution to ensuring the future security of democracies.

In "Politics as a Vocation," Weber says it is vital for leaders to find a balance between remaining true to their convictions, and taking responsibility for all the consequences of their acts. Those seeking to address problems related to political disengagement—declining voter turnout, rising mistrust of political elites, and loss of faith in representative democratic systems—might find "Politics as a Vocation" particularly useful.

NOTES

1   For the classic statement of this view, see Wolfgang Mommsen, *Max Weber and German Politics, 1890–1920* (Chicago: Chicago University Press, 1990).

2   See Russell J. Dalton, *Democratic Challenges, Democratic Choices: The Erosion of Political Support in Advanced Industrial Democracies* (Oxford: Oxford University Press, 2007).

3   See D. Runciman, *Political Hypocrisy: The Mask of Power, From Hobbes to Orwell and Beyond* (Princeton, NJ: Princeton University Press, 2008).

ACHIEVEMENT

KEY POINTS

- "Politics as a Vocation" is a greatly influential work on politics, power, the state, and political rule.

- The essay uses a concise, social-scientific method and draws from Weber's wider work to present an in-depth assessment of politics and political rule in twentieth-century Germany.

- It could be argued that the sheer amount of information condensed into the text, and the manner in which the information is presented, might make the text more difficult to appreciate.

Assessing The Argument

Max Weber wrote his essay "Politics as a Vocation" in an atmosphere of uncertainty. Germany was in the middle of a huge upheaval brought about by the country's defeat in World War I.* Two important left-wing politicians were assassinated only days before he was supposed to deliver his lecture at the University of Munich in January 1919. Weber refers to this climate, somewhat coyly, in the opening paragraph of "Politics as a Vocation:" "In a talk about politics as a vocation you will naturally expect to hear my opinions on topical questions."[1]

But Weber refused to offer his opinion on these specific issues. Instead, he employed the conceptual toolkit he had developed throughout his career to provide answers to basic questions about the nature of political action and its potential in general. Only once he had done this did he make some observations that were relevant to Germany's circumstances.

> ** ❝ Weber's discussion of the fate of politics in Germany, however intense its immediate engagement, always has implications for our fundamental understanding of the politics of the modern western state. ❞ **
>
> Peter Lassman and Roland Speirs, introduction to *Weber: Political Writings*

Addressing those seeking to act on the turbulent German political stage, the thrust of Weber's argument is that it would not be easy, and that Germany lacked leaders of the stature required to help it confront its crisis. It is not enough, he argued, to seek certain ends purely on the basis of one's convictions. Responsible politicians must take account of all the consequences of their actions, both intended and unintended. If the state is essentially a form of institutionalized violence, as Weber claims, then convictions or ethical drives are an insufficient basis for political action because politics necessarily involves using violence to achieve its ends.

Achievement In Context

Weber's lecture had a profound impact on his immediate audience. It was widely seen as a brilliant work, delivered by one of Germany's leading public intellectuals. The influence of "Politics as a Vocation" should therefore be seen in the light of Weber's own political standing and influence. He was a 1918 co-founder and prominent member of the German Democratic Party;* then, in 1919, he helped to draw up the first draft of the Weimar* Constitution, which set out the legal obligations and limits of Germany's new parliamentary republic.

The essay's lasting impact, meanwhile, can be attributed to Weber's refusal to engage with passing current events, despite their importance at the time, and instead to take the opportunity to deal with deeper structural issues.

Like the German philosopher Karl Marx* before him, Weber was concerned with the consequences of industrialization,* and the question of political rule given the decline of the traditional ruling classes. He was particularly interested in the impact of universal suffrage* (the right to vote) on the modern bureaucratic* state. His focus was on Germany, where the removal of a powerful and charismatic leader, Otto von Bismarck,* had, in his view, left a power vacuum which the German bourgeoisie* lacked the political education or maturity to fill.

His conclusions in "Politics as a Vocation," however, can be adapted to other modern developed nations. Indeed, much of the content of the lecture is drawn from the Great Britain and the United States, and he makes no claim to be talking exclusively about Germany.

Limitations

The sheer quantity of information packed into a short piece of writing may make the essay difficult to understand. Sections on the historical development of the state and of political parties in different countries require some prior knowledge if Weber's argument is to be fully appreciated. Even so, his writing style has a clarity that comes from his meticulous academic approach and his passion for the subject. Towards the end of the piece, Weber adopts a more fiery and literary tone to make his important point about the inner qualities that good politicians need.

Weber's understanding of how to conduct social science is obscure. But the essay had goals that may have made it difficult for Weber to explain his meaning clearly. In the opening paragraph, he states: "What will have to be completely ignored in the present talk will be all questions about the kind of politics that should be pursued, that is to say, the specific policies that should be adopted in the course of our political activities."[2] He claims not to offer any prescriptive statements, because of his commitment to keeping deliberately contentious views out of social science. Yet, contradicting this opening paragraph, the work *does* provide a normative approach* in its attempt to offer an account of how individuals ought to act politically—he does in fact suggest how things might or ought to be. Some critics consider this ambiguity to be a reflection of Weber's complex approach to the social sciences.

NOTES

1   Max Weber, "Politics as a Vocation," in *The Vocation Lectures*, eds. David Owen and Tracy B. Strong (Indianapolis, IN: Hackett, 2004), 32.

2   Weber, "Politics as a Vocation," 40.

MODULE 8
PLACE IN THE AUTHOR'S WORK

KEY POINTS

- "Politics as a Vocation" is a distillation of Max Weber's political thought. It draws on important concepts and arguments first seen in his earlier work.

- Weber's ideas were not fixed; they changed over time. His understanding of the best source of political leadership is just one example.

- Weber's work is interdisciplinary, reflecting his training. It addresses politics, economics, society, law, and religion.

Positioning

Max Weber died in 1920 at the age of 56, a year after his essay "Politics as a Vocation" was published. As a text written late in his life, and for a popular audience, it contains a succinct summary of many important aspects of the social and political thought that Weber developed in greater depth elsewhere.

In "Politics," Weber reprises arguments he had made as early as 1895, when he gave an address to Freiburg University that was later published as "The Nation State and Economic Policy." In this speech, Weber outlined his concept of German politics, noting the need for bureaucratic* organization to support democratic government, and Germany's lack of political leadership following the decline of the traditional ruling class.

Similar themes can also be found in a series of his essays published in one of Germany's most widely read newspapers, the *Frankfurter Zeitung*, in mid-1917.[1]

Weber's major work of social science, the unfinished *Economy and*

> ❝ The fifty-six years of his life saw the writing of an astonishing array of works, not only in the general field of political economy ... but also in philosophy, the methodology of social scientific investigation, musicology, the sociology of most of the world's major religions, social theory, and political science. ❞
>
> David Owen and Tracy B. Strong, *The Vocation Lectures*

Society,[2] contains many of the terms and concepts used in "Politics as a Vocation." This is perhaps not surprising, given that he wrote both texts over the same period. The shared concepts include his famous definition of the state as "the form of community that (successfully) lays claim to the monopoly of legitimate physical violence within a particular territory"[3] and his three "ideal types"* of legitimate authority: traditional,* legal,* and charismatic.*

The idea that the state should organize society rationally through bureaucracy to achieve stability and success, as expressed in "Politics as a Vocation," can be found in a less developed state in his important work *The Protestant Ethic and the Spirit of Capitalism* of 1905.*

Integration

Weber's other works discussing the history and nature of the modern* world contain a number of recurring themes that are taken up again in "Politics as a Vocation."

Perhaps the most important of these themes is the concept of rationalization.* For Weber, the distinctive feature of modernity is the increasing tendency for people in all walks of life to act rationally—in particular, to adopt the most efficient means of achieving their goals. This contrasts with behavior based on habit, tradition or emotion. For Weber, rationalization and the modern industrialized* age share many characteristics, notably "disenchantment:" the gradual replacement of social institutions and habits based on mystical and traditional beliefs with secular,* scientific norms and beliefs. A good deal of Weber's scholarship is concerned with charting the emergence and impact of this kind of rational thinking.

One of Weber's most famous works, *The Protestant Ethic and the Spirit of Capitalism*, examines how Protestant beliefs about material wealth contributed to the spread of rationality in economic life. It looks at how these beliefs eventually became a self-sustaining phenomenon that affected everyone who wanted to have a successful business—even those outside Protestant communities.

In "Politics," though, Weber explores a different aspect of rationalization: the way in which competition between powerful feudal* lords contributed to the emergence of a rationally organized bureaucratic state. According to Weber, the arrival of democratic competition drove other parts of the political system to bureaucratize.

Although there are important continuities in Weber's work, his thinking on certain subjects—his conception of the best source of political leadership, for example—changed over time. In the essay "Parliament and Government in a Reconstructed Germany" (1917),[4] Weber claimed that political leadership should emerge from parliament,* as in the British parliamentary model. However, in "Politics as a Vocation" and elsewhere in his work written after World War I,* he advocated a presidential system* in which the general public votes specifically for the winning candidate: "The only safety valve for the desire for leadership could be provided by the office of president of the [German nation] if the president were to be directly elected, instead of indirectly, by Parliament."[5] The reasons for his change of opinion have been a source of some controversy, and his shifting views were a precursor to later debates about the relative merits of parliamentary and presidential systems.

Significance

Given that it is a summary of the ideas Weber developed in more depth elsewhere, and also a text written for a popular audience, "Politics as a Vocation" has gained a wide readership but it is not its originality that makes it important.

Weber's two best-known texts are the books *The Protestant Ethic and the Spirit of Capitalism* and *Economy and Society.** The latter, published in 1922, two years after his death, is generally considered to be Weber's masterpiece and one of the most important sociological works of the twentieth century.[6]

The influence of Weber's body of work as a whole can be seen across the disciplines of sociology,* political science,* and economic history, and he remains one of the key figures in Western social science. But his most enduring influence has been on the methods used by scholars working in the social sciences. "Politics as a Vocation" is an example of this method at work.

In this context, the essay is significant for two reasons. First, it is a celebrated application of Weber's distinctive approach to social science. Most notably, in his discussion of legitimacy he uses an important conceptual tool—the ideal type—to analyze forms of legitimate authority. Ideal types are simplified depictions of a social phenomenon, which exaggerate essential aspects to help social scientists categorize and analyze the messy, complicated real world they are interested in. Here, Weber explains the emergence and nature of modern politics in terms of three kinds of ideal-typical authority: traditional, charismatic, and legal.

Second, Weber's outline of the historical development of political institutions clearly demonstrates his method of comparative and historical sociology.* Here, he explains the essential features of modern politics by comparing its historical emergence in a small number of countries.

Weber's method is still used by some historians and sociologists, notably historical/new institutionalists,* who use comparative history to explain the evolution of institutions. It is controversial among many academics, however, because it assumes that scientific knowledge of society must be based on interpretation or understanding,[7] in contrast to some of the principles of positivism* and neoclassical economics.* According to the positivist approach, knowledge of society comes solely from the analysis of observable phenomena. The theory of neoclassical economics, meanwhile, asserts that individuals always try to act rationally in pursuit of their own self-interest.

NOTES

1   A series of essays in the *Frankfurter Zeitung*, in Weber, *Economy and Society*, 1381–469.

2   Max Weber, *Economy and Society* (Berkeley: University of California Press, 1978).

3   Max Weber, "Politics as a Vocation," in *The Vocation Lectures*, eds. David Owen and Tracy B. Strong (Indianapolis, IN: Hackett, 2004), 33.

4   A series of essays in the *Frankfurter Zeitung*, in Weber, *Economy and Society*, 1381–469.

5   Weber, "Politics as a Vocation," 75.

6   For further details, see: International Sociological Association, "The Top 10 Books of the Century," accessed May 14, 2015, http://www.isa-sociology. org/books/books10.htm.

7   The German word Weber uses for "understanding" is *Verstehen*.

SECTION 3
IMPACT

MODULE 9
THE FIRST RESPONSES

KEY POINTS

- Since Weber died just a year after the essay's publication, there was no significant debate on "Politics as a Vocation" in his lifetime.

- The most important factors that shaped responses to the essay were the instability and polarization of Germany's political and social environment in 1919.

- Some might consider "Politics as a Vocation" to be dated, but Weber was right to say that bureaucratic* rules would dominate much of the political process in the future.

Criticism

The immediate response to "Politics as a Vocation" was very positive. Max Weber was one of the foremost public intellectuals of his day, and the lecture touched on matters of great importance at a time of huge political turmoil in Germany. As the Italian American sociologist* Gianfranco Poggi has written: "According to various witnesses, its original delivery as a lengthy talk to a large and restless audience constituted a breathtaking performance."[1]

As Weber died only a year after the lecture was published, in 1920, he had little time to engage with others on the ideas it expressed. Subsequent debate, when it did arise, focused on the essay's status within Weber's broader scholarship. Following his death, his work faded into relative obscurity for more than 30 years, especially in his native Germany where he was seen to represent an earlier, outmoded era. Given how influential Weber is now held to be, this is perhaps surprising.

> **❝** Weber's teachings concerning charismatic leadership coupled with the radical formulation of the meaning of democratic institutions, contributed to making the German people inwardly ready to acclaim the leadership position of Adolf Hitler. **❞**
>
> Wolfgang Mommsen, *Max Weber and German Politics: 1890–1920*

The earliest serious criticism of Weber's political thought emerged among German historians in the 1950s. Weber's biographer Wolfgang Mommsen* argued that his calls for strong leaders and a presidential system not only prepared the intellectual ground for Nazi* doctrine, but directly influenced the writing of the constitution of the Weimar Republic,* which facilitated the Nazis' rise to power in the 1930s.[2] The Hungarian Marxist* György Lukács* argued that Weber was part of a long tradition of bourgeois* German philosophy, stretching back to the influential G.W. F. Hegel* and Friedrich Nietzsche.* This tradition placed an emphasis on irrational forces such as charisma,* and ultimately led to the emergence of fascism.*

In the late 1960s, Marxists raised a second criticism of Weber's political thought, claiming that Weber's criticism of Karl Marx* confused cause and effect. Weber argued that rationalization* and bureaucratization* were fundamental features of modern society that affected capitalists* just as much as workers. Marxists such as the German American philosopher and sociologist Herbert Marcuse,* however, argued that these organizing principles were not neutral forces, but helped to underpin the power of capitalists.[3]

Responses

Although Weber did not live to hear or respond to these criticisms, they did draw a response from scholars sympathetic to his work. After his death, Weber's wife Marianne* pieced together his unfinished texts and published them as *Economy and Society** in the course of the 1920s. Yet despite her efforts to introduce her husband's work to a wider audience, Weber slid into relative obscurity.

Many scholars did not take his work seriously until the mid-1960s. Things had begun to change by 1964, however, when the German Sociological Association held a meeting to debate the importance of Weber's work. Key figures such as the American sociologist Talcott Parsons* and the French philosopher Raymond Aron* argued that his work was important. From that point on, Weber came to be regarded as one of the founders of sociology, alongside Karl Marx and the French sociologist Émile Durkheim.*

Parsons also played an important role in reviving interest in Weber's work thanks to his English translations and analyses. Later, renowned German academics such as the philosopher Jürgen Habermas* and the historian Wolfgang Mommsen discussed Weber's contributions, helping to restore his reputation.[4]

Claims that Weber laid the groundwork for Nazism are no longer uncritically accepted. More recent work has pointed out Weber's enduring, if sometimes qualified, commitment to liberalism.* As the British social theorist David Beetham has written: "Whatever the similarities [to fascist thought] in Weber's emphasis on strong leadership and national goals, he would have opposed many of the manifestations of Hitler's* rule: the total denial of civil liberties, the political interference in academic life, the racialist claptrap, the corporate state."[5].

Even Wolfgang Mommsen has accepted Weber's personal commitment to liberalism.

Finally, many commentators today consider that Weber's critique of Marx—in particular his claim that the establishment of a socialist economy would give rise to an even more powerful state bureaucracy—has been proved right by history.

Conflict And Consensus

Weber's political thought is no longer a matter of active contention among academics, largely because debates—indeed, the very terms of the debate, given developments in the field of sociological theory—have moved on.

Political scientists* may consider "Politics as a Vocation" to be a little dated. The world has changed since it was written, even if Weber was farsighted in his insistence that political parties and ministries or state departments are governed by the rules of bureaucracy, no matter what their ideological orientation.

The development of communist,* socialist,* and social-democratic* political parties in Europe over the course of the twentieth century have perhaps proved Weber correct. The essay, however, has little to say about why membership of political parties has declined so dramatically in recent decades, and why charismatic leaders seem unable to address the crisis facing so much of democratic politics.

Although Weber's analysis of authority remains an important point of reference, it does not directly inform a great deal of contemporary research among sociologists. In contrast with Weber's focus on why people consciously consent, a great deal of contemporary sociology focuses on how power operates *without* consent. Michel Foucault,* for example, a French historian of ideas and a celebrated social theorist in his own right, argued that modern institutions such as prisons and hospitals make sure people comply by ensuring they adopt value systems that favor particular kinds of behavior. In these cases, power "succeeds" by influencing the terms on which people decide whether or not to consent to commands from those in positions of formal authority. It should be noted, however, that while there are significant differences between Weber's and Foucault's analyses of power, there are also substantial similarities. For example, both agree that large bureaucratic institutions, which seek to control the behavior of the masses, characterize the modern world.

NOTES

1   Gianfranco Poggi, "*Wissenschaft als Beruf – Politik als Beruf*," *British Journal of Sociology* 45, no. 4 (2000): 720.

2   For the classic statement of this view, see Wolfgang Mommsen, *Max Weber and German Politics: 1890–1920* (Chicago: University of Chicago Press, 1984).

3   Herbert Marcuse, "Industrialisation and Capitalism in the Work of Max Weber," in *Negations: Essays in Critical Theory* (London: Penguin Press, 1968), 151–71.

4   Bernhard Schäfers, *Soziologie: Journal of the Deutsche Gesellschaft Für Soziologie* (Weisbaden: VS Verlag für Sozialwissenschaften, 2012), 116–19.

5   Beetham, *Max Weber and the Theory of Modern Politics* (London: George Allen & Unwin, 1974), 238–9.

MODULE 10
THE EVOLVING DEBATE

KEY POINTS

- Weber's understanding of the state as an organization that has a monopoly on legitimate force in a given territory is still the standard textbook definition in political science.

- Those who agree with Weber's vision of politics and society emphasize the importance of a strong state bureaucracy* and a charismatic* leader who can mobilize the masses towards stability and success.

- Scholars who are currently interested in Weber's work have looked to bring the role of the state back into focus in the study of political sociology.*

Uses And Problems

The conceptual tools, clear focus, and analytical methods Max Weber brought to bear in his political analysis—and which are exemplified in "Politics as a Vocation"—have all featured prominently in the scholarship that followed him.

Weber's analysis of the historical development of modern states has inspired many important thinkers, and some of his concepts are still relevant today. His definition of the state—an organization that enjoys a monopoly on legitimate force in a given territory—remains the standard textbook definition in political science. His distinction between the three types of legitimate authority (traditional,* charismatic, and rational-legal*), and his claim that rationalization* is key to understanding the modern* world, have all proven to be similarly influential, having inspired the work of social theorists such as Talcott Parsons,* a prominent mid-twentieth-century American

> **❝** Max Weber is perhaps the most troubling figure in twentieth-century social and political thought. His work has been the subject of widely differing interpretations and evaluations, from varying political and sociological standpoints. **❞**
>
> Donald A. Nielsen,* "The Question of Max Weber Today"

sociologist. Parsons has fallen from favor somewhat today—in part because he adopted a highly functionalist* perspective; this assumes that social phenomena exist in order to perform a "function" in a social system, and is an idea that most modern scholars consider to be flawed.

Weber's distinction between types of authority can still be seen in much of today's scholarship on public administration, particularly in the literature on leadership, even if few actually cite his work.

Many aspects of modern politics that Weber focused on in the essay remain prominent today. His comments on the bureaucratic nature of modern political parties, and his interest in the relationship between presidents* and parliaments,* were early examples of what has since become a large body of scholarship. In "Politics" Weber argues for a charismatic political leader elected by the people, with parliament offsetting the president's power and providing aspiring leaders with opportunities to gain a political education. This form of governance is now called a "semi-presidential" system.*

Debates around the relative merits of this and other constitutional systems continue. However, it should be noted that modern scholarship on these topics is diverse, and few modern political scientists would say that they work in a Weberian tradition.

Schools Of Thought

One school of thought directly inspired by Weber's political scholarship in general, and by "Politics as a Vocation" in particular, is the sub-field of democratic political theory called "competitive elitism"*[1] or "democratic elitism."*[2]

The main principle of elite theory is that political leadership lies at the heart of a democratic state. The general public's involvement in a democracy should be limited to selecting from among the elites, who compete for the right to govern. The theory also suggests that an extensive state bureaucracy is necessary for modern democracies. All these elements can be found in "Politics as a Vocation." After Weber, the Austrian American economist and political scientist, Joseph Schumpeter,* is the most important thinker in this tradition. Schumpeter developed a model of democracy that was explicitly intended to describe the way democratic societies are *actually* governed, rather than a utopian* ideal of how they ought to be.[3]

Over the years elite theory has evolved in many different ways. Although Weber and Schumpeter essentially endorsed elite rule as a practical necessity, others see it as an obstacle to true democracy. Many in this second group do agree, however, that the theory offers accurate descriptions of political realities.

The American sociologist C. Wright Mills,* for example, sought to show that power in the United States was actually exercised by a small number of elite groups drawn from big business, the military, and politics.[4] More recent schools of political thought also draw significant inspiration from Weber's work; these include theories of public policy that highlight the role of elites, such as corporatism* and policy network theory.*

In Current Scholarship

Weber's greatest influence on contemporary scholarship does not stem from his conceptual thinking or his clear interests but from his distinctive method. From the late 1970s, a small number of political sociologists working in the United States—among them Theda

Skocpol* and Michael Mann*—revived Weber's view that the state is worthy of study, because it is an important political actor in its own right.[5] In seeking to "bring the state back in" to political science, they differed from the two dominant strands of political thought in the United States at the time, which were Marxism* and pluralism.*

Marxism considers the state to be a tool of capitalist* interests, and not interesting in its own right; pluralism agrees, considering the state uninteresting because it implements policy in response to popular preferences, which are expressed via elections and lobbying by specific groups.

Political sociologists such as Skocpol and Mann argued that the evolution of important institutions, and policies such as social insurance and other welfare programs, could not be explained with either the Marxist or the pluralist approach. To make their case, they revived Weber's use of the comparative historical method*—that is to say, they compared the historical development of particular policies between nations and societies to identify important features that previous scholars had missed, having tended to focus on single countries such as the United States.

This use of comparative history to explain the evolution of institutions was given the name "historical institutionalism" or "new institutionalism."* It continues to be a small, but active and fruitful field of contemporary political and sociological research.

NOTES

1   D. Held, *Models of Democracy* (Palo Alto, CA: Stanford University Press, 2006).

2   P. Dunleavy and B. O'Leary, *Theories of the State: The Politics of Liberal Democracy* (Basingstoke: Macmillan, 1987).

3   Joseph Schumpeter, *Capitalism, Socialism and Democracy* (Abingdon: George Allen & Unwin, 2005).

4   C. Wright Mills, *The Power Elite* (Oxford: Oxford University Press, 2000).

5   See Theda Skocpol, "Bringing the State Back In: Strategies of Analysis in Current Research," in *Bringing the State Back In*, ed. Peter B. Evans, Dietrich Rueschemeyer, and Theda Skocpol (Cambridge: Cambridge University Press, 1985), 3–37.

MODULE 11
IMPACT AND INFLUENCE TODAY

KEY POINTS

- The essay "Politics as a Vocation" continues to have an important impact on academic debates about politics, power, the state, and political rule.

- Weber's text helps to fuel debate about exactly how much influence the general public can really have in the political landscape.

- "Politics as a Vocation" recognizes the real-life complications of political rule. Some people think that if the general public understood these difficulties better, this would help secure the future of democracy.

Position

Although it is safe to say that Max Weber's essay "Politics as a Vocation" has been a deeply influential text, the unique social and historical context in which the original lecture was given—the Germany of 1919—has meant that direct responses to it have often focused on the circumstances in which it was produced, or its position in Weber's wider corpus.

Another possible challenge to the essay's enduring relevance is Weber's focus on the importance of political leadership and the difficulties of political action. This perspective is often sidelined in the discipline of political science.* In seeking to explain political systems, political scientists have tended to focus on the behavior of institutions such as government, political parties, and the media and voters, rather than on the charisma of political leaders.* Although there are some

> **❝The prestige of Max Weber among European social scientists would be difficult to overestimate. He is widely considered the greatest of German sociologists and ... has become a leading influence in European and American thought. ❞**
>
> Hans Heinrich Gerth,* and C. Wright Mills,* introduction to
> *From Max Weber: Essays in Sociology*

exceptions, for much of the twentieth century there was little enthusiasm for discussing political leadership within the field.

Despite these challenges, Weber's scholarship has been revisited since the 1960s. Today he is widely regarded as one of the great sociologists* and thinkers of the social sciences. His views on politics, power, the state, and political rule remain influential, particularly in the field of political science.

Interaction

As a founding text of elite democratic theory,* "Politics as a Vocation" engages with several schools of thought. Most importantly, although many theorists of democracy believe there is value in people participating in government beyond simply voting, Weber consistently rejects this participation as unrealistic in modern mass society. The philosopher and sociologist Jürgen Habermas* was influenced by Weber's analysis, and argues that the rationalization* of society has restricted an individual's capacity to have a significant impact on public life.[1] However, while Weber sees this as an integral part of modern life that we must accept, Habermas says that it erodes democratic values, and is a problem that needs to be addressed. Like some other democratic theorists, Habermas does not accept Weber's assumption that elite rule* is inevitable, and that substantial involvement in public affairs on the part of the masses is impossible.

These debates tend to focus either on whether Weber described historical events accurately, or on whether his explanation for them was theoretically convincing. There is also another way that Weber's work can be approached. Ever since the classic analysis of Weber's thought by the German historian Wolfgang Mommsen,* Weber has been suspected of being part of the intellectual environment that allowed Nazism* to thrive in Germany in the 1920s and 1930s. Many political theorists—Habermas included—arguably seek to confront and overhaul Weber's pessimism about the nature of political rule in order to confront the dark history of the twentieth century.

The Continuing Debate

Some aspects of Weber's views on politics can be removed from their historical context and applied to current political problems. In this sense, they have universal value. Today, there is a widespread and growing mistrust of politicians and formal politics in developed democracies,[2] which some thinkers believe to be a serious threat to the future legitimacy and sustainability of democratic societies. This mistrust has been attributed, at least in part, to a misunderstanding of the nature of political rule and of the fact that politics really is a difficult and complicated occupation.

Some theorists, like the British political scientist, David Runciman,* suggest that a better recognition of these difficulties could help people to come to terms with the problems of democratic politics,[3] and make an important contribution to ensuring the future security of democracies.

In "Politics as a Vocation" Weber describes the delicate balancing act between an ethics of conviction* (that is, a belief in following one's convictions, combined with the view that morally, force is never justifiable) and an ethics of responsibility* (that is, the belief that politicians must react responsibly to changing conditions, and that force is sometimes necessary) that political leaders must manage.

The nature of leadership has changed little since Weber's original lecture of 1919, and this balancing act is still necessary. Those who want to address the issue of political disengagement—declining voter turnout, rising mistrust of political elites, and loss of faith in representative democratic systems—may do well to return to "Politics as a Vocation" to engage with Weber's reasoning.

NOTES

1   J. Habermas, *The Theory of Communicative Action: Reason and the Rationalization of Society* (Boston: Beacon Press, 1987).

2   See for example Russell Dalton, *Democratic Challenges, Democratic Choices: The Erosion of Political Support in Advanced Industrial Democracies* (Oxford: Oxford University Press, 2007).

3   See for example David Runciman, *Political Hypocrisy: The Mask of Power, from Hobbes to Orwell and Beyond* (Princeton, NJ: Princeton University Press, 2008).

WHERE NEXT?

KEY POINTS

- Max Weber's ideas on politics, power, the state, and political rule will continue to be an integral part of political science.

- It is likely that Weber's ideas will still be highly relevant at a time when faith in our political processes is constantly being questioned.

- "Politics as a Vocation" is a key text because it explains what politics is, how politics relates to power, and how politics and power evolve in relation to the modern* state, while also giving a definition of "good political leadership."

Potential

Max Weber delivered his 1919 lecture "Politics as a Vocation" in extraordinary social and political circumstances. Yet, even though some of the references may be obscure to the modern reader, the essay is still required reading for many introductory politics courses. Indeed, it could be argued that Max Weber's lecture has never been more relevant.

Many analysts are concerned that the increasing mistrust of politicians and political parties in modern democracies[1] is a real danger to the long-term security of democratic societies. This mistrust can be partly explained, perhaps, in terms of a general lack of understanding of the complications involved in governing. Some theorists suggest that the situation would be improved if the intricacies of democratic politics were more widely understood.[2] Weber outlines the difficult balance that politicians must maintain between an ethics of

> ❝ Weber is one of the few scholars of a century ago with whom most contemporary social scientists still feel the need to come to terms. ❞
>
> David Owen* and Tracy B. Strong,* introduction to *The Vocation Lectures*

conviction* and an ethics of responsibility,* a tightrope that leaders must still walk today.

Anyone addressing issues such as the decline in the number of citizens who register to vote, and rising skepticism about how government is run, will find plenty of relevant material in "Politics as a Vocation." Although Weber was alert to the historical context in which he was writing, his core thesis concerns the internal conditions for political action—and these do not change, regardless of circumstances.

Weber's specific analysis of the emergence of modern political institutions in certain countries, and their impact, may become dated. But his philosophical and theoretical statement about what it takes to "do politics well" should retain its relevance.

Future Directions

Max Weber's conceptualization of political leadership and the distinction he makes between "those who live for politics" and "those who live from politics" is likely to remain significant. He was highly skeptical of those who made a living from politics, and believed that Germany was in the middle of a deep crisis because of poor political leadership. Being a German nationalist,* Weber was concerned by the power of the United States and Great Britain, but also envied it. He believed that politics was not merely a job, but rather what he called a *beruf*: a calling, comparable to the callings answered by the prophets of the Old Testament.*

In Weber's view, politicians must maintain strong ethical values, while simultaneously seeing the world as it is and not how they would ideally, perhaps unrealistically, like it to be. In this sense, he very clearly opposed the utopianism* of Marxist* thought. Unlike Marx,* Weber saw bureaucracy* as the machinery of rule, and did not accept that this would change just because some other group—the working class, for example—happened to be in charge. Instead, he thought that leaders should be both able to serve at the head of a large organization, and possess personal qualities that inspire others to follow them. The enduring importance of these two characteristics—authority and charisma*—can still be recognized in recent political figures such as the former British Prime Minister Margaret Thatcher.*

At a time when voters are increasingly disillusioned with their leaders, failed public policies, and corruption, it seems likely that Weber's ideas will continue to speak to us.

Summary

Max Weber's essay "Politics as a Vocation" is important for its unusual breadth. It serves as a summary of Weber's political thought, using the conceptual toolkit, experience and knowledge he had gathered over his career to examine contemporary politics in both theory and in practice. Bearing the hallmarks of a text produced at an especially volatile moment in history, it offers a window into the social and political turmoil that marked Germany in January 1919. In summary, "Politics as a Vocation" presents the political thought of one of the founders of modern social science, at a time when he was particularly engaged in public affairs.

While Weber builds on much of the work of his contemporaries and predecessors in the essay, his philosophical contemplation of the inner conditions required for political action is built on original thought. The lecture also provides a classic example of the Weberian method, with its use of ideal types* and historical sociology.* As methodology is the field in which Weber is thought to have had the most influence, "Politics as a Vocation" remains valuable for this alone.

Despite the unusually volatile historical context in which it was produced, "Politics as a Vocation" is still relevant today. Although political leadership remains relatively unexplored in academic terms, good leadership is a prized quality and a desirable political goal, particularly in times of crisis. With faith in the representative systems of many developed democracies declining year by year, and with trust in politicians continuing to plummet,[3] "Politics as a Vocation" offers a uniquely powerful insight into the problems of political action in a democracy. Few other texts can be regarded as having so successfully demonstrated the complex bases on which political power is founded.

NOTES

1   See for example Russell Dalton, *Democratic Challenges, Democratic Choices: The Erosion of Political Support in Advanced Industrial Democracies* (Oxford: Oxford University Press, 2007).

2   See for example David Runciman, *Political Hypocrisy: The Mask of Power, from Hobbes to Orwell and Beyond* (Princeton, NJ: Princeton University Press, 2008).

3   Colin Hay, *Why We Hate Politics* (Cambridge: Polity Press, 2007).

GLOSSARY

GLOSSARY OF TERMS

American Revolution: a period of political upheaval in the late eighteenth century during which American colonists struggled against Great Britain to establish the United States of America.

Aristocracy: the highest level of society, sometimes but not always the ruling class. Aristocrats usually inherit their position.

Bourgeoisie: those who own and manage capitalist production. This ruling class is often seen as an oppressor of the working class.

Bureaucracy: a form of highly rational organization. Max Weber argued that bureaucracy was a distinctive feature of modernity, and a necessary part of the modern state.

Calvinist Protestantism: a form of Christian faith and practice that developed in opposition to the Roman Catholic Church. It follows the theological tradition of the French theologian and reformist John Calvin.

Capitalism: an economic system that emphasizes the private ownership of the means of production—those things, such as land, natural resources, and technology that are necessary for the production of goods.

Charismatic authority: a type of authority that occurs when people obey someone not because of tradition, or law, but because they identify with and believe in the leader. This was one of Max Weber's key concepts in "Politics as a Vocation."

Class consciousness: the awareness of one's place in a system of social classes. This is particularly relevant to the Marxist idea of class struggle.

Communism: a political ideology that relies on state ownership of the means of production (those things, such as land, natural resources, and technology that are necessary for the production of goods), the collectivization of labor, and the abolition of social class.

Comparative historical method: a method of social scientific analysis. It consists of comparing and contrasting the historical development of the institutions in a small number of different cases, usually countries. Weber is seen as one of the founders of this method.

Corporatism: a social system characterized by the organization of political society into large groups. It is particularly associated with attempts to describe many Western European political systems in the period after World War II, when labor, business, and the government were particularly significant in the governing of democratic states.

Divine rule: the idea that kings and queens have a God-given right to rule and that any form of rebellion is unjustifiable.

***Economy and Society*:** a book written by Max Weber. It was published in 1922 and is considered to be one of the most important sociological works of the twentieth century. In essence, it is a broad and detailed textbook on politics, society, religion, law, bureaucracy, charisma, and leadership.

Elitism (elite theory): a broad range of theories, which have in common the insistence that social affairs are (or even should be) controlled by small groups of elites.

Empiricism: the theory that people only learn things through their senses—in other words, via their experiences.

Enlightenment: "The Enlightenment" refers to a cultural and intellectual movement that sought to reform society through the use of reason. It is often accepted to have culminated in the French Revolution of 1789.

Ethics of conviction: an approach to politics that judges the rightness of political behavior by the moral worth of its goals, rather than the means employed to achieve them ("the end justifies the means").

Ethics of responsibility: an approach to politics that takes into account the actual consequences of actions, not just whether they are intended to achieve morally worthwhile things.

Fascism: a radical political ideology that privileges the unity and power of a nation or race over the flourishing of the individual by means of a centralized, authoritarian state that aims to suppress all opposition. It came to prominence in Europe in the 1920s and 1930s in such nations as Germany and Italy. Some scholars have argued that Max Weber's advocacy for strong, charismatic leaders contributed to the rise of fascism in Germany.

Feudalism: a system of government that was particularly widespread in Europe between the 800s and 1400s. At its core, feudalism was organized around a hierarchy, in which subordinates (vassals) held land on behalf of their lord in exchange for military service.

French Revolution: a period of deep political and social transformation in France between 1789 and 1799. It influenced the course of Western history as a whole.

Functionalism: an approach to social science that explains the existence of social phenomena in terms of their effects (that is, the function they fulfill in an overall social system). Functionalism was prominent among sociologists in the mid-twentieth century. It is no longer widely accepted or used.

German Democratic Party: a political party formed at the end of World War I. It argued for a democratic republic that would act in the national interest. It was dissolved in 1933 upon Adolf Hitler's accession to power.

German Empire: The German Empire was formed in 1871, when 27 German-speaking territories united under Prussian leadership. It was replaced by the Weimar Republic in 1918, when Kaiser Wilhelm II abdicated following defeat in World War I.

Hereditary succession: the transfer of power through inheritance. This occurs in a monarchical system of government.

Historical sociology: the scientific study of the historical development of societies. Weber is seen as the founding thinker of this branch of sociology.

Ideal type: a key element of Weberian methodology in social science. Ideal types are a little like caricatures: they are a simplified depiction of a social phenomenon, in which essential aspects are exaggerated and non-essential aspects are left out. Much like caricatures, they do not conform precisely to the real-world phenomenon they represent. Social scientists use ideal types as tools for rigorously and transparently categorizing and analyzing the messy, complicated real-world social phenomena they are interested in.

Idealism: the practice of envisioning society in an ideal or impractical form. Max Weber argued against this in his challenge to Marxism.

Industrialization: the process whereby a society moves from an agricultural system to one based on the production of goods and services.

Iron Law of Oligarchy: a theory proposed by Robert Michels, a former student of Max Weber. It argues that all organizations, including political parties, must inevitably be controlled by elites.

Kaiser: a German word meaning emperor. There were only three Kaisers of the German Empire (the German-speaking territories that agreed to come together under Prussian leadership), which existed between 1871 and 1918.

Legal authority: a key Weberian concept, also known as "rational-bureaucratic authority" and "rational-legal authority." It describes the authority that comes with holding a particular office, supported by a legal system.

Liberal democracy (liberal democratic theory): a form of government characterized by representative democracy and the protection of individual liberties under the law.

Liberalism: a political philosophy that assigns the utmost importance to individual freedom. This is of fundamental importance to the development of Western societies, and lies at the root of many of their institutions, values, and practices.

Marxism: the name given to the political system advocated by Karl Marx. It emphasizes an end to capitalism by taking control of the means of production (things such as land, natural resources, and technology that are necessary for the production of goods) from individuals and placing them in the hands of central government.

Modernity: a historical period that began in Europe in roughly the sixteenth century, and that continues to the present in many important respects. It is characterized by a particular combination of norms, attitudes and practices. These include an emphasis on individualism, freedom, reason and rationality, capitalism, industrialization, and secularization.

Monarchy: a state led by a sovereign head, which could be a king or a queen, for example, or the royal family to which that king or queen belongs.

National assembly: the elected legislature in some countries. At the time "Politics as a Vocation" was published, the German National Assembly was very unstable.

Nationalism: devotion to the interests of a particular nation-state. Max Weber was a German nationalist.

Nation-state: a state that, in theory, is comprised predominantly of common cultures, history, and languages.

Nazism: the extremely right-wing political philosophy instituted by Adolf Hitler in Germany from 1933 to 1945.

Neoclassical economics: an approach to economic analysis that assumes that people have known preferences that correspond with choices in the real world, and that they act rationally to satisfy those preferences in the most efficient way possible.

New institutionalism: a term describing the assumption that institutions are the correct unit of analysis in seeking explanations for social outcomes.

Normative statements: statements expressing value judgments; they state how things ought to be.

Old Regime: the French political and social system before the Revolution of 1789, which was characterized by aristocratic rule and hereditary succession.

Old Testament: the first part of the Bible, the sacred text of Christianity. Max Weber's understanding of charismatic authority was rooted in the idea that the prophets of the Old Testament were "called" to their vocation.

Parliament: a representative body having supreme legislative powers within a state. Max Weber believed that a parliament could provide the political education that would create great leaders.

Parliamentary system of government: a system of democratic governance in which the executive is drawn from, and nominally accountable to, the legislature (parliament). One of the best-known parliamentary systems is in Great Britain, where the executive consists of the prime minister and a number of other ministers (who are all members of parliament).

Pluralism: see pluralist system of democracy.

Pluralist system of democracy: a system of democratic governance in which power is shared between different elements of society, rather than there being just one center of power.

Policy network theory: a theory that seeks to explain the formation of public policy through the recognition that (often small) communities form around particular policies and are responsible for the direction those policies take.

Political science: a social science that focuses on political behavior and institutions. Weber's definition of "politics" in "Politics as a Vocation" implies that he considered political science to be the study of behavior oriented towards winning control of the state, and using its power.

Popular sovereignty: the principle that by electing representatives, the general population gives consent to the authority of the government. Max Weber opposed this in its purest form, as represented by the French Revolution of 1789.

Positivism: an approach to social science that believes knowledge of society can only be derived from directly observable phenomena, such as behavior. Positivists hold that phenomena that cannot be directly observed, such as beliefs, can only be studied indirectly through their impact on things that can be observed. Today, positivism is often associated with quantitative (i.e. statistical) social science. Weber was one of the founders of anti-positivist sociology, which focuses on understanding the beliefs of the people being studied.

Presidential system of government: a republican form of government in which the head of state leads the executive branch, which is separate from the legislature. This is the system operating in France and in the United States.

Proletariat: a term central to Marxist theory, virtually synonymous with "working class." Max Weber argued that elites should govern society, not the proletariat.

Protestant Work Ethic and the Spirit of Capitalism: a seminal text written by Max Weber, published in 1905. It argues that the modern capitalist system has its roots in the emergence of Calvinist Protestantism in Europe and North America.

Prussia: a former state in north-central Germany. Max Weber was born there.

Rationalization: A key Weberian concept, rationalization refers to the transition that takes place when a traditional community, organized on the basis of habitual action, evolves into a modern bureaucratic society, in which the legitimacy of authority rests on rational principles.

Rational-legal authority: see legal authority.

Realism: a philosophical attitude to reality according to which an individual accepts a situation the way it is and responds to it in a practical manner. Max Weber believed that political leaders must react to society the way it is, and not how they would idealistically like it to be.

Reichsbank: the central bank of Germany from 1876 until 1945. Max Weber refers to it in "Politics as a Vocation."

Religious doctrine: the systematic teaching of a particular religion, usually based on an agreed interpretation of one or more holy texts. Weber's most famous sociological analysis of doctrine is found in *The Protestant Ethic and the Spirit of Capitalism* (where he argues that Calvinist Protestantism contributed to the development of early capitalism in Europe).

Representative democracy: a form of government in which citizens, rather than making public decisions directly, elect a body of representatives who will then act in their name.

Republic (republican government): a republican government is one in which the head of government does not inherit the role, but obtains it by other means, most commonly through elections.

Secularism: a term for the belief that those with religious authority should not enjoy privileged access to political power. In the modern world, it is commonly associated with an institutional separation of the Church from the state, and the idea that people of different religions and beliefs are equal under the law. Max Weber believed that the decline of religion in the West had led to a widespread feeling of disenchantment in society.

Semi-presidential system: a system of government in which power is shared between a president and a prime minister. It is generally the president who is the head of state, and the prime minister who is head of the government.

Social Democratic Party: although this name has been used by political parties in different contexts, today, broadly speaking, social democratic parties espouse a political philosophy that holds that capitalism and socialism are compatible. The German Social Democratic Party took power in Germany shortly before Weber delivered the "Politics" lecture.

Socialism: the belief that society should be organized in such a way that the methods of production, distribution, and exchange are owned and regulated by the community as a whole, rather than by a select few.

Sociology: Sociology is the study of "social action." This means action that is oriented towards others—for example, because it seeks to have an impact on others, or because it anticipates how others might react to it. Weber was particularly interested in the meaning of social action.

Traditional authority: a key Weberian concept, this term designates authority that comes from respect for traditions or customs.

Treaty of Versailles: The peace treaty, signed in the French town of Versailles on June 28, 1919, which ended hostilities between Germany and the Allies in World War I. It imposed harsh economic and military terms on Germany, which caused great resentment, and because of this it is often said to have contributed to World War II.

Utopian: the model of a state in which everything is theoretically perfect. Max Weber believed that this characterized Marxism.

Weimar Republic: the constitutional German state that was formed following World War I. Theoretically, it existed until 1945, but it is more commonly thought to have ended with the coming to power of Adolf Hitler in 1933.

World War I: a war fought between 1914 and 1918. The Allies (Britain, France, Russia, and Italy) defeated the Central Powers (Germany, Austria-Hungary, Bulgaria, and the Ottoman Empire).

World War II: a war that occurred between 1939 and 1945. It was fought between the extremely right-wing regimes of Nazi Germany and Japan, and the Allies, which included Great Britain and the United States of America.

Universal suffrage: the extension of the right to vote to all (or at one time, all male) citizens.

PEOPLE MENTIONED IN THE TEXT

Aristotle (circa 384–322 b.c.e.) was a Greek philosopher and a founding intellectual of Western thought. His *Politics* is often seen as the first academic attempt to understand the political realm.

Raymond Aron (1905–83) was a French philosopher, sociologist and political scientist.

Benjamin Disraeli (1804–81) was a British conservative politician, twice elected as prime minister. He was a nationalist,* who championed Britain's aggressive role in foreign affairs.

Émile Durkheim (1858-1917) was a French sociologist, social psychologist and philosopher. He is widely considered to have been one of the founding fathers of sociology and social science, along with Karl Marx and Max Weber.

Michel Foucault (1926–84) was a French historian. His work on the emergence of institutions like the prison and the hospital, and on the associated practices of social control they embodied, has been extremely influential in a wide range of fields, including sociology, history, politics, and the law.

Hans Heinrich Gerth (1908–78) was an American sociologist of German descent. He was an expert on Max Weber.

William Gladstone (1809–88) was a charismatic British liberal politician who served as prime minister on four occasions.

Jürgen Habermas (b. 1929) is a lauded German philosopher and sociologist. He is author of *The Structural Transformation of the Public Sphere*, among other seminal works.

G. W. F. Hegel (1770–1831) was a German philosopher and author of *Phenomenology of Spirit*. He was enormously influential on a wide range of nineteenth- and twentieth-century European thinkers including, most notably, Karl Marx.

Adolf Hitler (1889–1945) was leader of the extremely right-wing National Socialist (Nazi)* Party and Chancellor of Germany, becoming dictator in 1934. Some scholars have claimed that Weber's advocacy for a strong, charismatic leader contributed to Hitler's rise to power.

Karl Jaspers (1883–1969) was an important German psychiatrist and philosopher. He attended Weber's "Politics as a Vocation" lecture in 1919 at the University of Munich.

Peter Lassman is a lecturer in political science at the University of Birmingham. He is an expert on Max Weber.

Karl Liebknecht (1871–1919) was a German socialist who co-founded the revolutionary Spartacus League, along with Rosa Luxemburg. He and Luxemburg were assassinated 13 days before the "Politics as a Vocation" lecture.

György Lukács (1885–1971) was a Hungarian Marxist philosopher, who made important contributions to Marxism. He argued that Weber's ideas paved the way for the rise of fascism* in Germany.

Rosa Luxemburg (1871–1919) was a Marxist thinker and writer, and an important figure in the development of German socialist thought and practice.

Niccolò Machiavelli (1469–1527) was the Italian author of *The Prince*, a foundational text in political science. He argues that politicians must use their charisma, and sometimes deceitful practices, in order to stay in power.

Michael Mann (b. 1942) is a British American sociologist at the University of California, Los Angeles. Max Weber's scholarship has influenced Mann's work.

Herbert Marcuse (1898-1979) was a German American Marxist philosopher, and social and political scientist. Marcuse was associated with the Frankfurt School of critical Marxism.

Karl Marx (1818–83) was an enormously influential German philosopher and social scientist, the author of *Capital* and *The Communist Manifesto*, who was a founding thinker in the development of socialism and communism.

Robert Michels (1876–1936) was a German sociologist and a founder of the school of elite theory. He was a former student of Weber's and influenced the author's views on political parties.

C. Wright Mills (1916–62) was an American sociologist and professor at Columbia University. His seminal work *The Power Elite* was influenced by the views of Max Weber.

Wolfgang Mommsen (1930–2004) was an expert on nineteenth- and twentieth-century German and British history. He wrote a biography on Max Weber in 1959.

Donald Nielsen is a lecturer in sociology at the University of Charleston in South Carolina and a Weber expert.

Friedrich Nietzsche (1844–1900) was a renowned German philosopher and intellectual. His scholarship influenced Max Weber's belief in the importance of heroic, charismatic leaders.

Moisei Ostrogorski (1854–1921) was a renowned Russian political scientist. His scholarship on political parties influenced Max Weber's views on bureaucratization.

David Owen is Professor of Social and Political Philosophy at the University of Southampton. He is an expert on the work of Max Weber.

Talcott Parsons (1902–79) was an American sociologist based at Harvard for almost 50 years. He received his PhD from Heidelberg, where he met Weber's wife Marianne. He went on to translate many of Weber's works into English.

Rainer Maria Rilke (1875–1926) was a renowned Bohemian Austrian poet. He attended Max Weber's "Politics as a Vocation" lecture at the University of Munich in 1919.

David Runciman (b. 1967) is an academic at Cambridge University, where he teaches political theory.

Joseph Schumpeter (1883–1950) was an Austrian American economist and political scientist known best in political science circles for his influence on the elitist school of thought. He, like Weber, shared an interest in the influence of political elites.*

Theda Skocpol (b. 1947) is an American sociologist and political scientist and professor at Harvard University. Max Weber has influenced her scholarship.

Tracy B. Strong is Distinguished Professor of Political Science at the University of California, San Diego. He is an expert on the scholarship of Max Weber.

Margaret Thatcher (1925–2013) was prime minister of the United Kingdom between 1979 and 1990. She is, it could be argued, an example of the Weberian concept of charismatic authority.

Otto von Bismarck (1815–98) was a German statesman widely regarded as the figure responsible for unifying Germany in 1871. Max Weber argued that his death left Germany lacking both a leader and a tradition of mature leadership.

Marianne Weber (1870–1954) was Max Weber's wife. Marianne was a sociologist and women's rights activist in her own right, and organized the publication of *Economy and Society** after Weber's death.

WORKS CITED

WORKS CITED

Beetham, David. *Max Weber and the Theory of Modern Politics*. London: George Allen & Unwin, 1974.

Dalton, Russell J. *Democratic Challenges, Democratic Choices: The Erosion of Political Support in Advanced Industrial Democracies*. Oxford: Oxford University Press, 2007.

Dunleavy, Patrick, and Brendan O'Leary. *Theories of the State: The Politics of Liberal Democracy*. Basingstoke: Macmillan, 1987.

Giddens, Anthony. *Politics and Sociology in the Thought of Max Weber*. London: Macmillan, 1972.

Habermas, Jürgen. *The Theory of Communicative Action: Reason and the Rationalization of Society*. Boston, MA: Beacon Press, 1987.

Hay, Colin. *Why We Hate Politics*. Cambridge: Polity Press, 2007.

Held, David. *Models of Democracy*. Palo Alto, CA: Stanford University Press, 2006.

Linz, Juan J. "Presidential or Parliamentary Democracy." In *The Failure of Presidential Democracy*, edited by Juan J. Linz and Arturo Valenzuela, 3–87. Baltimore, MD: John Hopkins University Press, 1994.

Marcuse, Herbert. "Industrialisation and Capitalism in the Work of Max Weber." In *Negations: Essays in Critical Theory*, London: Allen Lane, 1968.

Michels, Robert. *Political Parties: A Sociological Study of the Oligarchical Tendencies of Modern Democracy*. New Brunswick, NJ: Transaction Publishers, 1999.

Mills, C. Wright. *The Power Elite*. Oxford: Oxford University Press, 2000.

Mommsen, Wolfgang J. *The Age of Bureaucracy: Perspectives on the Political Sociology of Max Weber*. Oxford: Basil Blackwell, 1974.

Max Weber and German Politics, 1890–1920, translated by M. Steinberg. Chicago: University of Chicago Press, 1990.

Nietzsche, Friedrich. "Beyond Good and Evil." In *Basic Writings of Nietzsche*, translated and edited by Walter Kaufmann. New York: Modern Library, 2000.

Ostrogorski, Moisei. *Democracy and the Organisation of Political Parties*. New York: Haskell House, 1970.

Owen, David, and Tracy B. Strong. Introduction to *The Vocation Lectures*, edited by David Owen and Tracy B. Strong. Indianapolis, IN: Hackett, 2004.

Pateman, Carole. *Participation and Democratic Theory*. Cambridge: Cambridge University Press, 1975.

Poggi, Gianfranco. "*Wissenschaft als Beruf – Politik als Beruf.*" *British Journal of Sociology* 45, no. 4: 2000.

Runciman, David. *Political Hypocrisy: The Mask of Power, from Hobbes to Orwell and Beyond*. Princeton, NJ: Princeton University Press, 2008.

Schumpeter, Joseph. *Capitalism, Socialism and Democracy*. London and New York: Allen and Unwin, 2003.

Skocpol, Theda. "Bringing the State Back In: Strategies of Analysis in Current Research." In *Bringing the State Back In*, edited by Peter B. Evans, Dietrich Rueschemeyer, and Theda Skocpol, 3–37. Cambridge: Cambridge University Press, 1985.

Weber, Max. *Economy and Society*. Berkeley, CA: University of California Press, 1978.

"Politics as a Vocation." in *The Vocation Lectures*, edited by David Owen and Tracy B. Strong. Indianapolis, IN: Hackett, 2004.

Political Writings, edited by Peter Lassman and translated by Ronald Speirs Cambridge University Press, 1994.

THE MACAT LIBRARY
BY DISCIPLINE

The Macat Library By Discipline

AFRICANA STUDIES

Chinua Achebe's *An Image of Africa: Racism in Conrad's Heart of Darkness*
W. E. B. Du Bois's *The Souls of Black Folk*
Zora Neale Huston's *Characteristics of Negro Expression*
Martin Luther King Jr's *Why We Can't Wait*
Toni Morrison's *Playing in the Dark: Whiteness in the American Literary Imagination*

ANTHROPOLOGY

Arjun Appadurai's *Modernity at Large: Cultural Dimensions of Globalisation*
Philippe Ariès's *Centuries of Childhood*
Franz Boas's *Race, Language and Culture*
Kim Chan & Renée Mauborgne's *Blue Ocean Strategy*
Jared Diamond's *Guns, Germs & Steel: the Fate of Human Societies*
Jared Diamond's *Collapse: How Societies Choose to Fail or Survive*
E. E. Evans-Pritchard's *Witchcraft, Oracles and Magic Among the Azande*
James Ferguson's *The Anti-Politics Machine*
Clifford Geertz's *The Interpretation of Cultures*
David Graeber's *Debt: the First 5000 Years*
Karen Ho's *Liquidated: An Ethnography of Wall Street*
Geert Hofstede's *Culture's Consequences: Comparing Values, Behaviors, Institutes and Organizations across Nations*
Claude Lévi-Strauss's *Structural Anthropology*
Jay Macleod's *Ain't No Makin' It: Aspirations and Attainment in a Low-Income Neighborhood*
Saba Mahmood's *The Politics of Piety: The Islamic Revival and the Feminist Subject*
Marcel Mauss's *The Gift*

BUSINESS

Jean Lave & Etienne Wenger's *Situated Learning*
Theodore Levitt's *Marketing Myopia*
Burton G. Malkiel's *A Random Walk Down Wall Street*
Douglas McGregor's *The Human Side of Enterprise*
Michael Porter's *Competitive Strategy: Creating and Sustaining Superior Performance*
John Kotter's *Leading Change*
C. K. Prahalad & Gary Hamel's *The Core Competence of the Corporation*

CRIMINOLOGY

Michelle Alexander's *The New Jim Crow: Mass Incarceration in the Age of Colorblindness*
Michael R. Gottfredson & Travis Hirschi's *A General Theory of Crime*
Richard Herrnstein & Charles A. Murray's *The Bell Curve: Intelligence and Class Structure in American Life*
Elizabeth Loftus's *Eyewitness Testimony*
Jay Macleod's *Ain't No Makin' It: Aspirations and Attainment in a Low-Income Neighborhood*
Philip Zimbardo's *The Lucifer Effect*

ECONOMICS

Janet Abu-Lughod's *Before European Hegemony*
Ha-Joon Chang's *Kicking Away the Ladder*
David Brion Davis's *The Problem of Slavery in the Age of Revolution*
Milton Friedman's *The Role of Monetary Policy*
Milton Friedman's *Capitalism and Freedom*
David Graeber's *Debt: the First 5000 Years*
Friedrich Hayek's *The Road to Serfdom*
Karen Ho's *Liquidated: An Ethnography of Wall Street*

The Macat Library By Discipline

Eric Foner's *Reconstruction: America's Unfinished Revolution, 1863-1877*
Michel Foucault's *Discipline and Punish*
Michel Foucault's *History of Sexuality*
Francis Fukuyama's *The End of History and the Last Man*
John Lewis Gaddis's *We Now Know: Rethinking Cold War History*
Ernest Gellner's *Nations and Nationalism*
Eugene Genovese's *Roll, Jordan, Roll: The World the Slaves Made*
Carlo Ginzburg's *The Night Battles*
Daniel Goldhagen's *Hitler's Willing Executioners*
Jack Goldstone's *Revolution and Rebellion in the Early Modern World*
Antonio Gramsci's *The Prison Notebooks*
Alexander Hamilton, John Jay & James Madison's *The Federalist Papers*
Christopher Hill's *The World Turned Upside Down*
Carole Hillenbrand's *The Crusades: Islamic Perspectives*
Thomas Hobbes's *Leviathan*
Eric Hobsbawm's *The Age Of Revolution*
John A. Hobson's *Imperialism: A Study*
Albert Hourani's *History of the Arab Peoples*
Samuel P. Huntington's *The Clash of Civilizations and the Remaking of World Order*
C. L. R. James's *The Black Jacobins*
Tony Judt's *Postwar: A History of Europe Since 1945*
Ernst Kantorowicz's *The King's Two Bodies: A Study in Medieval Political Theology*
Paul Kennedy's *The Rise and Fall of the Great Powers*
Ian Kershaw's *The "Hitler Myth": Image and Reality in the Third Reich*
John Maynard Keynes's *The General Theory of Employment, Interest and Money*
Charles P. Kindleberger's *Manias, Panics and Crashes*
Martin Luther King Jr's *Why We Can't Wait*
Henry Kissinger's *World Order: Reflections on the Character of Nations and the Course of History*
Thomas Kuhn's *The Structure of Scientific Revolutions*
Georges Lefebvre's *The Coming of the French Revolution*
John Locke's *Two Treatises of Government*
Niccolò Machiavelli's *The Prince*
Thomas Robert Malthus's *An Essay on the Principle of Population*
Mahmood Mamdani's *Citizen and Subject: Contemporary Africa And The Legacy Of Late Colonialism*
Karl Marx's *Capital*
Stanley Milgram's *Obedience to Authority*
John Stuart Mill's *On Liberty*
Thomas Paine's *Common Sense*
Thomas Paine's *Rights of Man*
Geoffrey Parker's *Global Crisis: War, Climate Change and Catastrophe in the Seventeenth Century*
Jonathan Riley-Smith's *The First Crusade and the Idea of Crusading*
Jean-Jacques Rousseau's *The Social Contract*
Joan Wallach Scott's *Gender and the Politics of History*
Theda Skocpol's *States and Social Revolutions*
Adam Smith's *The Wealth of Nations*
Timothy Snyder's *Bloodlands: Europe Between Hitler and Stalin*
Sun Tzu's *The Art of War*
Keith Thomas's *Religion and the Decline of Magic*
Thucydides's *The History of the Peloponnesian War*
Frederick Jackson Turner's *The Significance of the Frontier in American History*
Odd Arne Westad's *The Global Cold War: Third World Interventions And The Making Of Our Times*

LITERATURE

Chinua Achebe's *An Image of Africa: Racism in Conrad's Heart of Darkness*
Roland Barthes's *Mythologies*
Homi K. Bhabha's *The Location of Culture*
Judith Butler's *Gender Trouble*
Simone De Beauvoir's *The Second Sex*
Ferdinand De Saussure's *Course in General Linguistics*
T. S. Eliot's *The Sacred Wood: Essays on Poetry and Criticism*
Zora Neale Huston's *Characteristics of Negro Expression*
Toni Morrison's *Playing in the Dark: Whiteness in the American Literary Imagination*
Edward Said's *Orientalism*
Gayatri Chakravorty Spivak's *Can the Subaltern Speak?*
Mary Wollstonecraft's *A Vindication of the Rights of Women*
Virginia Woolf's *A Room of One's Own*

PHILOSOPHY

Elizabeth Anscombe's *Modern Moral Philosophy*
Hannah Arendt's *The Human Condition*
Aristotle's *Metaphysics*
Aristotle's *Nicomachean Ethics*
Edmund Gettier's *Is Justified True Belief Knowledge?*
Georg Wilhelm Friedrich Hegel's *Phenomenology of Spirit*
David Hume's *Dialogues Concerning Natural Religion*
David Hume's *The Enquiry for Human Understanding*
Immanuel Kant's *Religion within the Boundaries of Mere Reason*
Immanuel Kant's *Critique of Pure Reason*
Søren Kierkegaard's *The Sickness Unto Death*
Søren Kierkegaard's *Fear and Trembling*
C. S. Lewis's *The Abolition of Man*
Alasdair MacIntyre's *After Virtue*
Marcus Aurelius's *Meditations*
Friedrich Nietzsche's *On the Genealogy of Morality*
Friedrich Nietzsche's *Beyond Good and Evil*
Plato's *Republic*
Plato's *Symposium*
Jean-Jacques Rousseau's *The Social Contract*
Gilbert Ryle's *The Concept of Mind*
Baruch Spinoza's *Ethics*
Sun Tzu's *The Art of War*
Ludwig Wittgenstein's *Philosophical Investigations*

POLITICS

Benedict Anderson's *Imagined Communities*
Aristotle's *Politics*
Bernard Bailyn's *The Ideological Origins of the American Revolution*
Edmund Burke's *Reflections on the Revolution in France*
John C. Calhoun's *A Disquisition on Government*
Ha-Joon Chang's *Kicking Away the Ladder*
Hamid Dabashi's *Iran: A People Interrupted*
Hamid Dabashi's *Theology of Discontent: The Ideological Foundation of the Islamic Revolution in Iran*
Robert Dahl's *Democracy and its Critics*
Robert Dahl's *Who Governs?*
David Brion Davis's *The Problem of Slavery in the Age of Revolution*

The Macat Library By Discipline

Alexis De Tocqueville's *Democracy in America*
James Ferguson's *The Anti-Politics Machine*
Frank Dikotter's *Mao's Great Famine*
Sheila Fitzpatrick's *Everyday Stalinism*
Eric Foner's *Reconstruction: America's Unfinished Revolution, 1863-1877*
Milton Friedman's *Capitalism and Freedom*
Francis Fukuyama's *The End of History and the Last Man*
John Lewis Gaddis's *We Now Know: Rethinking Cold War History*
Ernest Gellner's *Nations and Nationalism*
David Graeber's *Debt: the First 5000 Years*
Antonio Gramsci's *The Prison Notebooks*
Alexander Hamilton, John Jay & James Madison's *The Federalist Papers*
Friedrich Hayek's *The Road to Serfdom*
Christopher Hill's *The World Turned Upside Down*
Thomas Hobbes's *Leviathan*
John A. Hobson's *Imperialism: A Study*
Samuel P. Huntington's *The Clash of Civilizations and the Remaking of World Order*
Tony Judt's *Postwar: A History of Europe Since 1945*
David C. Kang's *China Rising: Peace, Power and Order in East Asia*
Paul Kennedy's *The Rise and Fall of Great Powers*
Robert Keohane's *After Hegemony*
Martin Luther King Jr.'s *Why We Can't Wait*
Henry Kissinger's *World Order: Reflections on the Character of Nations and the Course of History*
John Locke's *Two Treatises of Government*
Niccolò Machiavelli's *The Prince*
Thomas Robert Malthus's *An Essay on the Principle of Population*
Mahmood Mamdani's *Citizen and Subject: Contemporary Africa And The Legacy Of Late Colonialism*
Karl Marx's *Capital*
John Stuart Mill's *On Liberty*
John Stuart Mill's *Utilitarianism*
Hans Morgenthau's *Politics Among Nations*
Thomas Paine's *Common Sense*
Thomas Paine's *Rights of Man*
Thomas Piketty's *Capital in the Twenty-First Century*
Robert D. Putman's *Bowling Alone*
John Rawls's *Theory of Justice*
Jean-Jacques Rousseau's *The Social Contract*
Theda Skocpol's *States and Social Revolutions*
Adam Smith's *The Wealth of Nations*
Sun Tzu's *The Art of War*
Henry David Thoreau's *Civil Disobedience*
Thucydides's *The History of the Peloponnesian War*
Kenneth Waltz's *Theory of International Politics*
Max Weber's *Politics as a Vocation*
Odd Arne Westad's *The Global Cold War: Third World Interventions And The Making Of Our Times*

POSTCOLONIAL STUDIES

Roland Barthes's *Mythologies*
Frantz Fanon's *Black Skin, White Masks*
Homi K. Bhabha's *The Location of Culture*
Gustavo Gutiérrez's *A Theology of Liberation*
Edward Said's *Orientalism*
Gayatri Chakravorty Spivak's *Can the Subaltern Speak?*

PSYCHOLOGY

Gordon Allport's *The Nature of Prejudice*
Alan Baddeley & Graham Hitch's *Aggression: A Social Learning Analysis*
Albert Bandura's *Aggression: A Social Learning Analysis*
Leon Festinger's *A Theory of Cognitive Dissonance*
Sigmund Freud's *The Interpretation of Dreams*
Betty Friedan's *The Feminine Mystique*
Michael R. Gottfredson & Travis Hirschi's *A General Theory of Crime*
Eric Hoffer's *The True Believer: Thoughts on the Nature of Mass Movements*
William James's *Principles of Psychology*
Elizabeth Loftus's *Eyewitness Testimony*
A. H. Maslow's *A Theory of Human Motivation*
Stanley Milgram's *Obedience to Authority*
Steven Pinker's *The Better Angels of Our Nature*
Oliver Sacks's *The Man Who Mistook His Wife For a Hat*
Richard Thaler & Cass Sunstein's *Nudge: Improving Decisions About Health, Wealth and Happiness*
Amos Tversky's *Judgment under Uncertainty: Heuristics and Biases*
Philip Zimbardo's *The Lucifer Effect*

SCIENCE

Rachel Carson's *Silent Spring*
William Cronon's *Nature's Metropolis: Chicago And The Great West*
Alfred W. Crosby's *The Columbian Exchange*
Charles Darwin's *On the Origin of Species*
Richard Dawkin's *The Selfish Gene*
Thomas Kuhn's *The Structure of Scientific Revolutions*
Geoffrey Parker's *Global Crisis: War, Climate Change and Catastrophe in the Seventeenth Century*
Mathis Wackernagel & William Rees's *Our Ecological Footprint*

SOCIOLOGY

Michelle Alexander's *The New Jim Crow: Mass Incarceration in the Age of Colorblindness*
Gordon Allport's *The Nature of Prejudice*
Albert Bandura's *Aggression: A Social Learning Analysis*
Hanna Batatu's *The Old Social Classes And The Revolutionary Movements Of Iraq*
Ha-Joon Chang's *Kicking Away the Ladder*
W. E. B. Du Bois's *The Souls of Black Folk*
Émile Durkheim's *On Suicide*
Frantz Fanon's *Black Skin, White Masks*
Frantz Fanon's *The Wretched of the Earth*
Eric Foner's *Reconstruction: America's Unfinished Revolution, 1863-1877*
Eugene Genovese's *Roll, Jordan, Roll: The World the Slaves Made*
Jack Goldstone's *Revolution and Rebellion in the Early Modern World*
Antonio Gramsci's *The Prison Notebooks*
Richard Herrnstein & Charles A Murray's *The Bell Curve: Intelligence and Class Structure in American Life*
Eric Hoffer's *The True Believer: Thoughts on the Nature of Mass Movements*
Jane Jacobs's *The Death and Life of Great American Cities*
Robert Lucas's *Why Doesn't Capital Flow from Rich to Poor Countries?*
Jay Macleod's *Ain't No Makin' It: Aspirations and Attainment in a Low Income Neighborhood*
Elaine May's *Homeward Bound: American Families in the Cold War Era*
Douglas McGregor's *The Human Side of Enterprise*
C. Wright Mills's *The Sociological Imagination*

The Macat Library By Discipline

Thomas Piketty's *Capital in the Twenty-First Century*
Robert D. Putman's *Bowling Alone*
David Riesman's *The Lonely Crowd: A Study of the Changing American Character*
Edward Said's *Orientalism*
Joan Wallach Scott's *Gender and the Politics of History*
Theda Skocpol's *States and Social Revolutions*
Max Weber's *The Protestant Ethic and the Spirit of Capitalism*

THEOLOGY

Augustine's *Confessions*
Benedict's *Rule of St Benedict*
Gustavo Gutiérrez's *A Theology of Liberation*
Carole Hillenbrand's *The Crusades: Islamic Perspectives*
David Hume's *Dialogues Concerning Natural Religion*
Immanuel Kant's *Religion within the Boundaries of Mere Reason*
Ernst Kantorowicz's *The King's Two Bodies: A Study in Medieval Political Theology*
Søren Kierkegaard's *The Sickness Unto Death*
C. S. Lewis's *The Abolition of Man*
Saba Mahmood's *The Politics of Piety: The Islamic Revival and the Feminist Subject*
Baruch Spinoza's *Ethics*
Keith Thomas's *Religion and the Decline of Magic*

COMING SOON

Chris Argyris's *The Individual and the Organisation*
Seyla Benhabib's *The Rights of Others*
Walter Benjamin's *The Work Of Art in the Age of Mechanical Reproduction*
John Berger's *Ways of Seeing*
Pierre Bourdieu's *Outline of a Theory of Practice*
Mary Douglas's *Purity and Danger*
Roland Dworkin's *Taking Rights Seriously*
James G. March's *Exploration and Exploitation in Organisational Learning*
Ikujiro Nonaka's *A Dynamic Theory of Organizational Knowledge Creation*
Griselda Pollock's *Vision and Difference*
Amartya Sen's *Inequality Re-Examined*
Susan Sontag's *On Photography*
Yasser Tabbaa's *The Transformation of Islamic Art*
Ludwig von Mises's *Theory of Money and Credit*

Macat Disciplines

Access the greatest ideas and thinkers across entire disciplines, including

Postcolonial Studies

Roland Barthes's *Mythologies*
Frantz Fanon's *Black Skin, White Masks*
Homi K. Bhabha's *The Location of Culture*
Gustavo Gutiérrez's *A Theology of Liberation*
Edward Said's *Orientalism*
Gayatri Chakravorty Spivak's *Can the Subaltern Speak?*

Macat analyses are available from all good bookshops and libraries.

Access hundreds of analyses through one, multimedia tool.

Join free for one month **libra****: macat.com**

Macat Disciplines

Access the greatest ideas and thinkers across entire disciplines, including

AFRICANA STUDIES

Chinua Achebe's *An Image of Africa: Racism in Conrad's Heart of Darkness*

W. E. B. Du Bois's *The Souls of Black Folk*

Zora Neale Hurston's *Characteristics of Negro Expression*

Martin Luther King Jr.'s *Why We Can't Wait*

Toni Morrison's *Playing in the Dark: Whiteness in the American Literary Imagination*

Macat analyses are available from all good bookshops and libraries.

Access hundreds of analyses through one, multimedia tool. Join free for one month **library.macat.com**

Macat Disciplines

Access the greatest ideas and thinkers across entire disciplines, including

FEMINISM, GENDER AND QUEER STUDIES

Simone De Beauvoir's
The Second Sex

Michel Foucault's
History of Sexuality

Betty Friedan's
The Feminine Mystique

Saba Mahmood's
The Politics of Piety: The Islamic Revival and the Feminist Subject

Joan Wallach Scott's
Gender and the Politics of History

Mary Wollstonecraft's
A Vindication of the Rights of Woman

Virginia Woolf's
A Room of One's Own

Judith Butler's
Gender Trouble

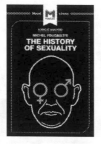

Macat analyses are available from all good bookshops and libraries.

Access hundreds of analyses through one, multimedia tool.

Join free for one month **library.macat.com**

Macat Disciplines

Access the greatest ideas and thinkers across entire disciplines, including

CRIMINOLOGY

Michelle Alexander's
*The New Jim Crow:
Mass Incarceration in the
Age of Colorblindness*

**Michael R. Gottfredson
& Travis Hirschi's**
A General Theory of Crime

Elizabeth Loftus's
Eyewitness Testimony

**Richard Herrnstein
& Charles A. Murray's**
*The Bell Curve: Intelligence and
Class Structure in American Life*

Jay Macleod's
*Ain't No Makin' It:
Aspirations and Attainment in a
Low-Income Neighborhood*

Philip Zimbardo's
The Lucifer Effect

Macat Disciplines

Access the greatest ideas and thinkers across entire disciplines, including

INEQUALITY

Ha-Joon Chang's, *Kicking Away the Ladder*

David Graeber's, *Debt: The First 5000 Years*

Robert E. Lucas's, *Why Doesn't Capital Flow from Rich To Poor Countries?*

Thomas Piketty's, *Capital in the Twenty-First Century*

Amartya Sen's, *Inequality Re-Examined*

Mahbub Ul Haq's, *Reflections on Human Development*

Macat analyses are available from all good bookshops and libraries.

Access hundreds of analyses through one, multimedia tool.

Join free for one month **library.macat.com**

Macat Disciplines

Access the greatest ideas and thinkers across entire disciplines, including

GLOBALIZATION

Arjun Appadurai's, *Modernity at Large: Cultural Dimensions of Globalisation*

James Ferguson's, *The Anti-Politics Machine*

Geert Hofstede's, *Culture's Consequences*

Amartya Sen's, *Development as Freedom*

Macat Disciplines

Access the greatest ideas and thinkers across entire disciplines, including

MAN AND THE ENVIRONMENT

The Brundtland Report's, *Our Common Future*
Rachel Carson's, *Silent Spring*
James Lovelock's, *Gaia: A New Look at Life on Earth*
Mathis Wackernagel & William Rees's, *Our Ecological Footprint*

Macat Disciplines

Access the greatest ideas and thinkers across entire disciplines, including

THE FUTURE OF DEMOCRACY

Robert A. Dahl's, *Democracy and Its Critics*
Robert A. Dahl's, *Who Governs?*
Alexis De Toqueville's, *Democracy in America*
Niccolò Machiavelli's, *The Prince*
John Stuart Mill's, *On Liberty*
Robert D. Putnam's, *Bowling Alone*
Jean-Jacques Rousseau's, *The Social Contract*
Henry David Thoreau's, *Civil Disobedience*

Macat Disciplines

Access the greatest ideas and thinkers across entire disciplines, including

TOTALITARIANISM

Sheila Fitzpatrick's, *Everyday Stalinism*
Ian Kershaw's, *The "Hitler Myth"*
Timothy Snyder's, *Bloodlands*

Macat Pairs

Analyse historical and modern issues from opposite sides of an argument. Pairs include:

RACE AND IDENTITY

Zora Neale Hurston's
Characteristics of Negro Expression

Using material collected on anthropological expeditions to the South, Zora Neale Hurston explains how expression in African American culture in the early twentieth century departs from the art of white America. At the time, African American art was often criticized for copying white culture. For Hurston, this criticism misunderstood how art works. European tradition views art as something fixed. But Hurston describes a creative process that is alive, ever-changing, and largely improvisational. She maintains that African American art works through a process called 'mimicry'—where an imitated object or verbal pattern, for example, is reshaped and altered until it becomes something new, novel—and worthy of attention.

Frantz Fanon's
Black Skin, White Masks

Black Skin, White Masks offers a radical analysis of the psychological effects of colonization on the colonized.

Fanon witnessed the effects of colonization first hand both in his birthplace, Martinique, and again later in life when he worked as a psychiatrist in another French colony, Algeria. His text is uncompromising in form and argument. He dissects the dehumanizing effects of colonialism, arguing that it destroys the native sense of identity, forcing people to adapt to an alien set of values—including a core belief that they are inferior. This results in deep psychological trauma.

Fanon's work played a pivotal role in the civil rights movements of the 1960s.

Macat analyses are available from all good bookshops and libraries.

Access hundreds of analyses through one, multimedia tool.
Join free for one month **library.macat.com**

Macat Pairs

*Analyse historical and modern issues
from opposite sides of an argument.
Pairs include:*

INTERNATIONAL RELATIONS IN THE 21ST CENTURY

Samuel P. Huntington's
The Clash of Civilisations
In his highly influential 1996 book, Huntington offers
a vision of a post-Cold War world in which conflict
takes place not between competing ideologies but
between cultures. The worst clash, he argues, will be
between the Islamic world and the West: the West's
arrogance and belief that its culture is a "gift" to the
world will come into conflict with Islam's obstinacy and
concern that its culture is under attack from a morally
decadent "other."

Clash inspired much debate between different political
schools of thought. But its greatest impact came in
helping define American foreign policy in the wake of
the 2001 terrorist attacks in New York and Washington.

Francis Fukuyama's
The End of History and the Last Man
Published in 1992, *The End of History and the Last Man*
argues that capitalist democracy is the final destination
for all societies. Fukuyama believed democracy
triumphed during the Cold War because it lacks the
"fundamental contradictions" inherent in communism
and satisfies our yearning for freedom and equality.
Democracy therefore marks the endpoint in the
evolution of ideology, and so the "end of history."
There will still be "events," but no fundamental
change in ideology.

Macat analyses are available from all good bookshops and libraries.

Access hundreds of analyses through one, multimedia tool.
Join free for one month **library.macat.com**

Macat Pairs

*Analyse historical and modern issues
from opposite sides of an argument.
Pairs include:*

HOW TO RUN AN ECONOMY

John Maynard Keynes's
*The General Theory OF Employment,
Interest and Money*

Classical economics suggests that market economies are self-correcting in times of recession or depression, and tend toward full employment and output. But English economist John Maynard Keynes disagrees.

In his ground-breaking 1936 study *The General Theory*, Keynes argues that traditional economics has misunderstood the causes of unemployment. Employment is not determined by the price of labor; it is directly linked to demand. Keynes believes market economies are by nature unstable, and so require government intervention. Spurred on by the social catastrophe of the Great Depression of the 1930s, he sets out to revolutionize the way the world thinks

Milton Friedman's
The Role of Monetary Policy

Friedman's 1968 paper changed the course of economic theory. In just 17 pages, he demolished existing theory and outlined an effective alternate monetary policy designed to secure 'high employment, stable prices and rapid growth.'

Friedman demonstrated that monetary policy plays a vital role in broader economic stability and argued that economists got their monetary policy wrong in the 1950s and 1960s by misunderstanding the relationship between inflation and unemployment. Previous generations of economists had believed that governments could permanently decrease unemployment by permitting inflation—and vice versa. Friedman's most original contribution was to show that this supposed trade-off is an illusion that only works in the short term.

Macat analyses are available from all good bookshops and libraries.

Access hundreds of analyses through one, multimedia tool.
Join free for one month **library.macat.com**

Macat Pairs

Analyse historical and modern issues from opposite sides of an argument. Pairs include:

ARE WE FUNDAMENTALLY GOOD - OR BAD?

Steven Pinker's
The Better Angels of Our Nature

Stephen Pinker's gloriously optimistic 2011 book argues that, despite humanity's biological tendency toward violence, we are, in fact, less violent today than ever before. To prove his case, Pinker lays out pages of detailed statistical evidence. For him, much of the credit for the decline goes to the eighteenth-century Enlightenment movement, whose ideas of liberty, tolerance, and respect for the value of human life filtered down through society and affected how people thought. That psychological change led to behavioral change—and overall we became more peaceful. Critics countered that humanity could never overcome the biological urge toward violence; others argued that Pinker's statistics were flawed.

Philip Zimbardo's
The Lucifer Effect

Some psychologists believe those who commit cruelty are innately evil. Zimbardo disagrees. In *The Lucifer Effect*, he argues that sometimes good people do evil things simply because of the situations they find themselves in, citing many historical examples to illustrate his point. Zimbardo details his 1971 Stanford prison experiment, where ordinary volunteers playing guards in a mock prison rapidly became abusive. But he also describes the tortures committed by US army personnel in Iraq's Abu Ghraib prison in 2003—and how he himself testified in defence of one of those guards. committed by US army personnel in Iraq's Abu Ghraib prison in 2003—and how he himself testified in defence of one of those guards.

Macat analyses are available from all good bookshops and libraries.

Access hundreds of analyses through one, multimedia tool.

Join free for one month libra██ macat.com

Macat Pairs

*Analyse historical and modern issues
from opposite sides of an argument.
Pairs include:*

HOW WE RELATE TO EACH OTHER AND SOCIETY

Jean-Jacques Rousseau's
The Social Contract

Rousseau's famous work sets out the radical concept of the 'social contract': a give-and-take relationship between individual freedom and social order.

If people are free to do as they like, governed only by their own sense of justice, they are also vulnerable to chaos and violence. To avoid this, Rousseau proposes, they should agree to give up some freedom to benefit from the protection of social and political organization. But this deal is only just if societies are led by the collective needs and desires of the people, and able to control the private interests of individuals. For Rousseau, the only legitimate form of government is rule by the people.

Robert D. Putnam's
Bowling Alone

In *Bowling Alone*, Robert Putnam argues that Americans have become disconnected from one another and from the institutions of their common life, and investigates the consequences of this change.

Looking at a range of indicators, from membership in formal organizations to the number of invitations being extended to informal dinner parties, Putnam demonstrates that Americans are interacting less and creating less "social capital" – with potentially disastrous implications for their society.

It would be difficult to overstate the impact of *Bowling Alone*, one of the most frequently cited social science publications of the last half-century.

Printed in the United States
by Baker & Taylor Publisher Services